Hotels to Remember

Hotels to Remember

Mary Montague Sikes

Oak Tree Publishing
In the Arts Colony 🌳 *Pomona, California*

Oak Tree Publishing

Oak Tree books may be purchased for educational, business, or sales promotional use. Contact Publisher for quantity discounts.

First Edition, July 2002
Printed in Korea

10 9 8 7 6 5 4 3 2 1

Sikes, Mary Montague
Hotels to remember / Mary Montague Sikes
P.cm
Includes bibliographical references

ISBN 1892343-18-5
1. Hotels—United States—Guidebooks.
2. Hotels—Canada—Guidebooks. I. Title.

TX907.2.S54-2002
647.9473'01—dc21   2001052039

Preface and Acknowledgements

Hotels to Remember has evolved almost on its own from a multitude of travel experiences and from my ever-growing fascination with memorable places and the wonderful hotels that make them special. The first hotel I found and loved was the El Tovar. Situated by the edge of the Grand Canyon, the El Tovar has a glorious, ever-changing, always magnificent view.

Like the El Tovar the other hotels in my book have a unique presence that make them unforgettable for me. Some have a tie with history and their own story to tell. Others have a bond with their communities that make them irreplaceable. A few have developed worldwide fame and a following of guests who return year after year.

Many people have helped make *Hotels to Remember* possible. The publicity directors, historians, and other personnel at each hotel have been wonderful and helpful. They have made available every resource I have requested. They have permitted me to photograph areas not always open to the public. They have returned my telephone calls and answered a multitude of questions. City convention centers and visitors bureaus also have proved invaluable resources.

As the book developed my publisher, Billie Johnson, and I spent many hours in the lobby of La Quinta Inn, Ontario, California viewing hundreds of slides and photographs. We studied possible book layouts and edited text. My thanks to Billie for her creative ideas and determination to make this project a success.

My special gratitude goes to Pierre Courtois who used his amazing talents to scan my photographs and photograph my paintings for *Hotels to Remember*. Thanks, too, to Petie Bogen-Garrett for her suggestions and advice on this project.

Most of all, my thanks go to Olen, my husband and dedicated partner in the production of this book. Without his steadfast support, *Hotels to Remember* would not exist.

As I brought this project to completion, I made the amazing discovery there are even more wonderful hotels old and new that I have not yet painted and about which I have not yet written. Please look for them coming soon in *More Hotels to Remember*.

Mary Montague Sikes

Foreword

All the hotels featured in Mary Montague Sikes' book have one very important thing in common that distinguishes them from their competitors in the marketplace. While most hotels today are parts of major chains, these are notable in their distinctiveness. While their "chained" competitors can be seen from city to city, each pretty much the same, these hotels are "one of a kind" and thus are memorable in and of themselves.

The great chain hotels (and there are many) remind visitors of the same hotel they stayed at in another city. The great hotels featured here remind visitors of the city they were in, as much as the hotel they were in. They do so because they are a part of the fabric of the community. They reflect its people, its culture, its values, its atmosphere. They are run and populated by people who are permanent residents of the community and care for it deeply.

These hotels generally become a "labor of love" for their owners. Many have been under the same ownership for generations. Often the management and the ownership are one and the same—not very typical anymore. These owners have discovered they possess real "treasures" that are impossible to duplicate. They also discover that owning a hotel entails wear and tear under the best of circumstances. And to keep them distinctive and worthy of the special trust their communities place in them requires constant infusions of time, money and tender loving care. These owners think about return on investment, but practice preservation of irreplaceable assets in equal measure, knowing that in the long term they are priceless.

Most importantly, they recognize their hotels play a central role in their community's every day life. Their lobbies are where local residents and visitors gather, their restaurants the dining rooms where they entertain their guests and their bedrooms, of course, where their guests sleep. These are the places where visitors come to understand what the community is all about.

Central to that are its people. The owners of these hotels take special care to recruit, train and retain the very best of the community's citizens. These owners know the reason visitors stay at their hotels is because their staffs take special pride in their community and in the hotel that represents its very essence. They are every bit as important as the bricks and mortar in making these Hotels to Remember.

Stephen Marcus,
The Marcus Corporation
Milwaukee, Wisconsin

Table of Contents

Hotels to Remember

Part I

Hotels of the Mid-Atlantic

Hotel Jefferson, 20 by 26 inches, original pastel by Mary Montague Sikes.

Hotel Jefferson Tower, 26 by 20 inches, original pastel by Mary Montague Sikes.

Hotel Jefferson ~ Named for a Hero

For well over a century the Hotel Jefferson has stood as a lustrous sentinel between Main and Franklin Streets—a Richmond, Virginia landmark. Periodically circumstances have led to the hotel closing for renovations and repairs, yet invariably the basic structure and the interior have remained imposing. Today, as it did more than a century ago, the Hotel Jefferson symbolizes a vision and represents an American hero: Thomas Jefferson, third president of the United States.

The opening of the Jefferson in 1895 satisfied the grand purposes of Major Lewis Ginter who came to Richmond as an 18-year-old in 1842. The son of Dutch immigrants, Ginter served in the Confederate Army during the Civil War. He had been a fabric merchant, eventually became a wealthy tobacco businessman, and then a land developer. His vision was to build the "finest hotel in America" and to name it after Thomas Jefferson, the American patriot who was his hero and a true "Renaissance man."

He hired the New York architectural firm of Carrerre and Hastings of New York City for the project and commissioned artist Edward V. Valentine to create a Carrara marble statue of Jefferson. An oil painting Ginter purchased, "The Soap Bubbles," by Elizabeth Gardner Bouguereau, first exhibited at the 1893 World's Columbian Exposition in Chicago, continues on display today at its original site on the wall of the Lemaire Restaurant Library.

The architects designed an eclectic composite of Renaissance and other architectural styles popular at the turn of the 20th Century. Today, the Jefferson Hotel in Richmond is held to be one of the finest existing examples of the Beaux-Arts style.

From opening day on October 31, 1895, the Jefferson featured the modern amenities of hot and cold running water, electric lights, even elevators. Palm trees were brought in from South America, along with antiques from throughout the world. Money went a ways in those days but Ginter still spent about $8 million on the structure and furnishings.

The Jefferson actually opened ahead of schedule so as to accommodate the wedding guests of the socialite beauty Irene Langhorne and Charles Dana Gibson, a Richmond resident. The November 7 wedding was the social event of the year, itself a magnet for prominent out-of-town visitors.

At its opening the Jefferson, "a fitting tribute to American architectural genius," was acclaimed as "the most magnificent hotel in the south and unsurpassed in the north." Unfortunately Ginter failed to enjoy his creation for long. He died in 1897.

In 1901 a disastrous fire ruined about 60 per cent of the structure. The Thomas Jefferson statue was almost a casualty of the fire, but a rescue team managed to save the huge marble artwork by toppling it onto mattresses. In the process the head was broken off and remained in a neighborhood yard for several days until the sculptor, Edward Valentine, retrieved it for repair. Eventually Valentine reattached the head and the statue was returned to its place in the hotel lobby.

This marble statue of Thomas Jefferson, sculpted by Edward V. Valentine, is the focal point of the Hotel Jefferson lobby. The statue originally was installed in The Rotunda at the University of Virginia, the institution founded by Mr. Jefferson. Nine sections of the domed 35-foot stained glass skylight are original Tiffany.

Although the Franklin Street portion of the Jefferson reopened a few months after the fire, in its damaged state the facility was considerably diminished in size and luster. Eventually a group of business entrepreneurs formed the Jefferson Realty Corporation and began a restoration project that rebuilt the Rotunda, the mezzanine and Grand Staircase, all in the portion closed off following the fire. Renovation of the Franklin Street side of the hotel and the addition of the Grand Ballroom wing were part of the $1.5 million project designed by architect J. Kevan Peebles.

The Jefferson had its Grand Reopening on May 6, 1907.

Presidents Harrison, McKinley, Wilson, Coolidge, Taft, Theodore Roosevelt, Franklin D. Roosevelt, Truman, and Reagan all have been guests. Other notables who have stayed there include Sarah Bernhardt, John Denver, Helen Hayes, Elvis Presley, Frank Sinatra, and the rock group Chicago.

Bill (Bojangles) Robinson, born and raised nearby and celebrated for his dancing on stairs and street corners, worked as a dining room server at the Jefferson where he met the movie producer who would become his manager.

As with other old hotels, the Jefferson began a gradual decline during World War II. Management contracted to house military recruits, and air raid regulations led to the removal of stained glass from the ceilings. A second fire in 1944 further added to the demise of the facility that eventually shut its doors in 1980.

The Jefferson remained closed for six years, then—as part of the Sheraton Hotel chain—reopened on May 6, 1986, following a $34 million, three-year restoration project. In 1991, a Richmond investor group, Historic Hotels, Inc., bought the Jefferson and spent an additional five million on renovations.

A $3 million project in 1999 created a covered motor court entry, indoor pool, and a glass conservatory addition to the Lemaire Restaurant. Another $1.5 million was spent upgrading guestrooms and interior public spaces.

Following these renovations, in 2000 and 2001 the Hotel Jefferson earned the Mobil Travel Guide's five-star award for two straight years, one of only 25 hotels in the continental United States and Canada to achieve this rating in the annual guide published by Exxon Mobil Corporation. The Jefferson was also named a five-diamond hotel by the Automobile Association of America.

Today the life–size statue of Jefferson still graces the European–style Palm Court Lobby. A spectacular 35-foot Tiffany stained glass skylight stretches in Art Deco elegance above the statue's head—a fitting tribute to President Jefferson and to Lewis Ginter's vision of a grand hotel.

Hotel Jefferson exterior view following renovations in 2000

Alligators in the Lobby

About the time of the Grand Reopening of the Hotel Jefferson between 1905 and 1907, live alligators were placed in the sunken rills beside the Thomas Jefferson statue in the Palm Court.

According to legend and other reports, the alligators were given or left by guests who acquired them as pets on trips to Florida. They eventually found that their "pets" required too much space in family bathtubs or were not exactly what they had expected.

Containers of alligators sometimes could be found at the registration desk or in the Rotunda. The story goes that a bellman might enter the hotel to go on duty in the early morning and actually find the alligators lounging on the fine furniture where guests would later sit. It became part of the daily routine to run the alligators off the seats and back into the water.

Old Pompey, the last of those alligators, died in 1948, and the fountains where they lived are gone from the lobby.

Hotel Jefferson as it appeared in 1999 prior to renovations

Hotel Jefferson Towers

The twin towers of the Hotel Jefferson are among its most striking features. Rising 150 feet from the ground, each tower has three faces of a clock that measure more than six feet across. The pendulums inside are more than 13 feet long.

According to a newspaper report, in December, 1954, Allen Baringer, a 12-year-old sixth grader, received permission to inspect the clocks that had been silent for many years. The youngster's examination revealed that steel parts inside the clocks had rusted and that pigeons were using the spaces for roosts.

Patiently, young Allen greased and oiled the frozen parts and soon had the clocks running again.

At the beginning of the new 21st century, visitors to Richmond still pause and regard with awe the imposing Jefferson Hotel towers. The towers create an image worth remembering. No wonder they inspired young Allen Baringer.

The Stairway Legend

The long stairway leading up to the lobby of the Jefferson Hotel has fired many an imagination to believe it was the model for the elegant staircase in *Gone With the Wind.* Over the years, quite a few Richmond residents have encouraged their guests to believe in the legend. Visiting the Jefferson's small museum next to the staircase, you can find at least two newspaper articles about the legend. One in the November 11, 1976, edition of the *Richmond Times-Dispatch* claims the "grand" staircase was the model for the stairs in the mansion in the movie setting. The story quotes D. T. Oakes, hotel general manager at the time.

However, another well-displayed article claims otherwise. In a column of December 18, 1990, in the *Richmond News Leader*, newspaper writer Steve Clark reports interviewing Lyle Reynolds Wheeler, art director for *Gone with the Wind.* During that interview Clark quotes Wheeler as saying the movie stairway was not a copy of any "existing structure."

Some believe the staircase legend grew out of a hotel marketing ploy that probably generated much interest when the movie was reaching the height of its popularity. Even so, the long, wide stairway carpeted in rich red remains a symbol of grandeur for the historic Jefferson, a place where once, long ago, Southern Belles gathered to display their wit and charm in hopes of attracting a husband.

Nowadays as the Hotel Jefferson grows in quality and services, the romance and legend of the staircase live on.

Over the years, many people believed that the dramatic staircase leading up to the lobby in the Hotel Jefferson served as the model for the elegant stairs in, "Gone with the Wind."

Hotel Roanoke ~ *Roanoke, Virginia*

Hotel Roanoke, 20 by 26 inches, original pastel by Mary Montague Sikes.

Hotel Roanoke ~ Coming Back to Family

Making guests feel welcome is the goal of most hotels. Making them feel at home is even better. For more than a century, the Hotel Roanoke has had a reputation for doing both.

"I felt like family coming back home," one guest observes, remembering her many stays there.

"It has comfortable elegance," she says, her face brightening with a nostalgic smile. "The hotel staff was always very gracious."

Elegance, grace, charm, and comfort are qualities repeat guests at the Hotel Roanoke have come to expect and to anticipate. They also relish the historic connection the hotel has with the local community—a connection that continues today.

When guests go into the spacious lobby and discover the comfortable setting with its dark wooden paneling, they sense entering another era. It is the year 1882, and Roanoke is the little town of Big Lick with a population of less than 700 people.

That was one year after railroad magnate Frederick J. Kimball made his decision to select Big Lick as the site of the crossing of the north-south Shenandoah Valley Railroad and the east-west Atlantic, Mississippi & Ohio. The railroads were combined to create the Norfolk and Western. Kimball also decided to promote the idea of creating a major city at Big Lick and building a "grand hotel," as well as houses and shops.

George Pearson, a Philadelphia architect, was hired to design the structure—a Queen Anne-style, mostly wooden hotel. The building site, chosen by Kimball, was a wheat field situated on a slight hill overlooking the railroad tracks. The 177 foot-long by 73 foot-wide structure was built at a cost of about $60,000 and featured the most up-to-date amenities, including hot and cold running water in all guestrooms. The new hotel celebrated its official opening on Christmas Day, 1882.

The location next to a railroad connecting North, South, East, and Midwest allowed the hotel, from its beginning, to draw a broad range of travelers, including those who needed a break in their tiring train trips. Guests included business people, and, especially in the summertime, vacationers coming to enjoy the mountain air.

The dining room where a lavish nine-course meal had been served on opening day was an attraction in itself. Up to 200 people could dine at one time beneath elegant chandeliers and near beautiful hand-polished wooden panels. The Blue Ridge Mountains provided a spectacular backdrop to the "grand hotel" and could be seen from most windows and doors.

In 1898, much of the hotel was destroyed by fire; however, following the completion of extensive repairs, it reopened a few months later. Over the next few decades the Hotel Roanoke added new wings and additions. In 1916, the east wing was replaced with a three-story, 72-room section. In 1931, a $225,000 building project added 75 rooms and a 60-car garage.

A more costly $1,050,000 remodeling project in 1938 included construction of the imposing Tudor entrance that distinguishes the hotel today. The elegant porches, where many a young lady had sat and rocked enjoying the mountain air and watching passersby, were removed and 181 rooms added. Additional public rooms included the Regency Room, home of elegant breakfast dining and the peanut soup that chef Fred Brown created in 1940, and the Pine Room, a paneled pub that served as a World War II Officers Club. The new guestrooms boasted of air conditioning, tiled tub and shower, venetian blinds, and circulating ice water.

Amelia Earhart, Jeanette MacDonald, Joe DiMaggio, and Jack Dempsey were among the many celebrated hotel guests. Presidents Ronald Reagan, Jimmy Carter, George Bush, Richard Nixon, Gerald Ford, and Dwight David Eisenhower all spent nights at the Hotel Roanoke. Many Virginians can recall good times at the hotel when they attended high school Beta Club conventions, state Jaycee meetings, and many other similar functions. Others recall attending the Virginia Junior Miss pageant or the Miss Virginia pageant, both featured for many years at the Hotel Roanoke.

A prized photograph in Donlan Piedmont's book, *Peanut Soup and Spoonbread: An Informal History of the Hotel Roanoke,* shows Governor Mills Godwin seated with six former Virginia Governors, all of whom were there to celebrate the hotel's 85th birthday in 1967. The former governors who attended were: Thomas B. Stanley, John S. Battle, William M. Tuck, Colgate W. Darden, Albertis S. Harrison, and J. Lindsay Almond.

Throughout its history, the hotel ballroom often

overflowed with exotic and lavish flower arrangements when it served as the setting for flower shows, wedding receptions, and private parties. In the 1960s, the ballroom was the site of a cattle auction. Today the hotel continues to host such functions and to serve as the center for political conventions and numerous government meetings.

For a time, it was feared that the colorful history of Hotel Roanoke would end for good. Since the hotel, despite it good reputation and service, was losing money and had to be subsidized, the Norfolk Southern Corporation (product of a merger between Norfolk & Western and Southern Railway) decided to close the hotel and donate it to Virginia Tech to be used for conferences and continuing education.

On November 30, 1989, the hotel closed its doors to guests; then, for 17 days in December, everything from chandeliers and lobby bar down to silverware and dishes was auctioned off. During those auctions, representatives of Center in the Square, a popular arts center near the hotel, were able to purchase six dozen table-settings and many other items useful for receptions.

After the closing, the city of Roanoke and Virginia Tech worked to raise funds to finance renovations and the construction of an adjacent 63,000-square-foot conference center. The "Renew Roanoke" campaign was created and successfully raised, through private and public funding, $27.5 million for the renovation. Norfolk Southern gave $2 million to the fund, while Doubletree Hotels made a $1.3 million loan for the project. Personalized bricks laid outside the hotel entrance helped raise some of the funding.

On April 3, 1995, Hotel Roanoke reopened under the management of Doubletree Hotels and "in partnership with Virginia Tech." With 332 guestrooms and a covered pedestrian walkway leading to the historic downtown area, the hotel once again displays the charm and presence of old.

Standing graciously on its low hill, overlooking the city and railroad, the hotel again welcomes guests and seeks to make them feel at home. Once more the Hotel Roanoke claims its title as the Grand Old Lady of Roanoke.

During a 1938 remodeling projects, porches were removed and replaced by the Tudor entrance seen today.

Dark paneling and comfortable furnishings in the lobby invite guests at the Hotel Roanoke to linger.

Hotel Roanoke (seen from the back) was built in 1882 where a wheat field once stood.

Williamsburg Inn, 26 by 20 inches, original pastel by Mary Montague Sikes.

Williamsburg Inn ~ An Historic Destination

Those who live in or near Williamsburg, Virginia glory in the unforgettable atmosphere of history and colonial charm spread out over the city. The Historic Area—stretching from the College of William and Mary at one end of Duke of Gloucester Street to the Capitol building at the other—attracts droves of admiring visitors from all over the world. Nearby, at the edge of the restored area, the Williamsburg Inn offers gracious accommodations, graceful décor, and delightful gourmet dining.

An unexpected quiet greets arriving guests as they pull into the big oval driveway that leads to the Williamsburg Inn. Tall white portico columns and a long row of lower arches add to the welcoming grandeur of a southern mansion. The bright red, white, and blue colors of three flags—the Stars and Stripes, the Virginia Flag, and the Colonial Williamsburg flag—all wave proudly above the distinctive white-washed brick entrance.

The lobby is furnished in the Regency style of early nineteenth century England, a contrast to the largely Georgian period décor of the Historic Area. Guests enjoy the unique, individual touches John D. Rockefeller, Jr. and Abby Aldrich Rockefeller personally added to Williamsburg Inn. Wanting the Inn to possess the welcoming appeal of a comfortable, cozy home, the Rockefeller couple became involved not only in design and construction but also in the selection of furnishings.

The story goes that on one occasion Mrs. Rockefeller was dissatisfied with the lobby's appearance, so she brought in some help and spent several hours completely rearranging the furniture into a more inviting configuration. Today, more or less as Mrs. Rockefeller placed it years ago, crimson upholstered furniture sits beneath a gleaming crystal prism chandelier in the lobby, encouraging guests to relax in the home-like atmosphere and chat with friends.

An oval handmade rug in the lobby is an exact replica of the one the Rockefellers purchased for the Inn. The original rug is in storage, having been replaced when it began to show wear. Photographs,

The Williamsburg Inn, as viewed from the golf course behind, reveals a more traditional colonial facade.

scaled patterns of design elements, and fiber clippings were sent to China to ensure that the hand-hooked copy would be an exact replica.

Arched French doors opposite the lobby entrance allow guests to observe the seasonal flowering of azaleas, dogwoods, and magnolia trees that flourish in Virginia. The doors open onto a wide flagstone terrace furnished with stylish garden tables and chairs.

Oil portraits of people important to Williamsburg's past cover the walls of public areas. Prints and drawings of European vistas decorate hallways and corridors.

Williamsburg Inn goes back to 1926 when Dr. W. A. R. Goodwin, the forward-thinking rector of Bruton Parish Church, disclosed his plans for the restoration of eighteenth-century Williamsburg to John D. Rockefeller, Jr. Responding to the rector's vision of returning the town to its early glory, Rockefeller made plans to support the project. Soon after restoration began, the need for a suitable place for guests to stay while visiting the area became apparent.

Colonial Inn, a twentieth century building then sitting where Chowning's Tavern now stands, was acquired and refurbished. With only 21 guestrooms, it opened in 1931 as the Williamsburg Inn. However, the building was not large enough to house many guests, and its location in the middle of the Historic Area became a problem for those who did not want to keep a twentieth century building in the restoration area. Another colonial building, the Market Square Tavern, was adapted for guest accommodations and also opened in 1931.

In 1935, a site on Francis Street near the Historic Area boundary was selected for construction of a new Inn that would offer the "wide variety of recreational amenities found at leading American resorts." Colonial Williamsburg Hotel Properties proposed making the Inn a "complete, self-contained resort as a destination for guests," and building of the new facility began in April 1936.

Unlike the usual eighteenth century restored area, Architect William G. Perry sought a unique style for the Inn "that would set it apart." Since Virginia for years had been noted for its heated springs, Perry selected a

heated mineral springs hotel, Old Sweet, in Sweet Springs, West Virginia (close to the Virginia border) to serve as guide for the "character" of Williamsburg Inn.

On April 3, 1937, the Williamsburg Inn, with 61 well-appointed guest rooms, held its grand opening. Just prior to the official opening, the American Institute of Decorators became the first group to hold a conference at the Inn. That was the beginning of the Inn's long and admirable reign as one of Virginia's best known hotels. Since 1994, the Inn has been listed as one of only five Virginia hotels included in the directory of *Historic Hotels of America*.

During World War II, like many other hotels across the nation, Williamsburg Inn faced difficult times. Since nearly all its guests came by car, the Inn

Bright flags above the front entrance of Williamsburg Inn add a splash of color against the white exterior.

Buildings in the restored area of colonial Williamsburg attract droves of visitors year round

staircase. Boneless breast of chicken with Virginia ham was on one of the menus served the royal couple during that celebrated visit.

Historically it has become commonplace for national and world leaders to arrive in Williamsburg to stay at the Inn. In 1983, an economic summit was held in Williamsburg, with guests including President and Mrs. Ronald Reagan, Canadian Prime Minister Pierre Trudeau, French President Francois Mitterand, British Prime Minister Margaret Thatcher, and other world leaders.

Today there are accommodations for 95 guestrooms, decorated in the Regency style, while the Providence Hall wings (not connected to the main Inn) offer some of the area's best convention facilities.

The Regency Dining Room, added in 1972 to accommodate 184 diners, is well known throughout the region for elegant dining. Lavish decorations include crystal chandeliers, leather chairs, hand-painted Chinese silk wallpaper, and silk draperies. On a busy day the chef and his staff of 60 may serve as many as 1200 meals. Mouth-watering pecan tarts and the Governor's chocolate torte are favorite desserts at the Inn. Recreation gets a high priority at Williamsburg Inn. In 1963, with the increasing popularity of golf, Colonial Williamsburg built an 18-hole championship golf course. The Golden Horseshoe Golf Course, considered his "finest design," was planned by Robert Trent Jones, Sr.

suffered from a lack of patrons beginning in early 1942 when gasoline rationing curtailed pleasure driving. To aid in the war effort, rooms at the Inn were rented to officers stationed in the area to train draftees at Fort Eustis and Camp Peary. It was not until 1946 that the Williamsburg Inn once again opened its doors to the general public.

Since then, there have been decades of distinguished visitors, including Winston Churchill and General Dwight D. Eisenhower in March, 1946. In October 1957, to commemorate the 350th anniversary of the settlement at Jamestown, Queen Elizabeth II and Prince Philip stayed at the Inn in a second floor suite now called, of course, the Queen's Suite. The queen, an attractive young woman wearing a diamond tiara and elaborate white satin gown, was photographed descending the curved East Wing

Incorporating some of the natural trees with flowering plants, Jones created a colorful course that spreads over 125 acres behind the Inn's south terrace. A five-acre lake seems par for the course. A second championship golf course, designed by the Jones' son, Rees, opened in 1992. The Golden Horseshoe Green Course that he created is reminiscent of Scotland golf courses and features "sculptured mounding along the edges of the fairways" and "elaborate bunkering." At the time, the original Golden Horseshoe Course was renamed the Golden Horseshoe Gold Course. Renovations to the Williamsburg Inn, completed in September 2001, converted 100 small rooms into 62 luxury suites. The work closed portions of the Inn for several months in late 2000 and early 2001. The new units have doubled in size, growing to 500 square feet. Some seventy percent of the furniture removed

from the Inn was refinished and reupholstered for use in the new rooms. Draperies were cleaned for reuse, as well as many other items including closet doorknobs. Marble bathrooms now have modern whirlpools and separate showers.

Despite all of the changes to the infrastructure and technology, the look of the Williamsburg Inn remains unchanged. The idea is that return guests continue to feel right at home when they glimpse the tree-lined drive and see the flag-draped front entrance. Many visitors come to Williamsburg to enjoy special themed events such as the February Antique Forum, Garden Week in April, or the Christmas Illumination. The Inn offers memorable accommodations and hospitality year round. With the Historic Area only a short walk away, guests have access to America's early history and to a unique shopping experience without moving a car.

Neatly arranged gardens adorn the restored area of Colonial Williamsburg.

A Side Trip to James River Houses

Ghosts and History Ply Banks of James River

Tales of ghosts fascinate us. So do beautiful old mansions. On the banks of the James River between Williamsburg and Richmond, visitors to the historic area will discover three memorable plantation houses and perhaps the ghosts that haunt them.

Evelynton, built in 1737, is one of the newest plantations. Overlooking the James, the rambling brick manor house offers some of the area's most colorful history, including reported ghost sightings.

Much of the historic interest surrounding the plantation owes to the feats of Edmund Ruffin whose son, Edmund Ruffin, Jr., purchased Evelynton at auction in 1847. The senior Ruffin, a renowned Virginia planter, earned the title, "father of American agronomy." He later gained notoriety as a major promoter of states rights. Perhaps for that reason, he was designated to fire the first Civil War shot at Fort Sumter, South Carolina in 1861.

Historians believe that because of what Ruffin did, Evelynton was particularly hard hit during the war. Site of some of the most fierce fighting of the Seven Days Battle between Confederate troops, led by J.E.B. Stuart, and Union forces, the mansion and its out-buildings were plundered and burned.

Tales of Evelynton's ghost began in an earlier period, during the eighteenth century, when the property was part of Westover Estate then owned by William Byrd II. As described by tour guides and by L. B. Taylor, Jr. in *The Ghosts of Tidewater*, the ghost at Evelynton is said to be that of Byrd's beautiful, heart-broken daughter.

Evelyn Byrd, born in 1707, was to have inherited Evelynton. Instead, she made the mistake of falling in love with a man of whom her father disapproved. The romance began while the young woman was in England to receive her education and to be presented at the court of King George I. The man with whom she fell in love was Charles Mordaunt, a grandson of the Earl of Peterborough and a Catholic by faith. Byrd, a Protestant, is reported to have objected to Mordaunt for religious reasons. He brought Evelyn back to Virginia where it is said she was never again

With a little imagination one might discern the ghostly image of Evelyn Byrd peering through a window at beautiful Evelynton Plantation.

The portrait known as "Aunt Pratt" once again hangs at Shirley Plantation. According to stories passed along for many years, the portrait caused a great deal of trouble in the household when it was removed from the wall and stored in the attic. Some claimed that the sounds of relentless rocking mysteriously began occurring on certain nights. Eventually, when the portrait was returned to the wall, the rocking noises were heard no more.

Since its opening to the public in 1986, Evelynton has proven a popular destination for those who enjoy visiting historic houses. Today the 2500-acre working farm with its Georgian Revival manor house is often the site of receptions and, as well, the setting for major television commercials.

The Ruffin family still resides in the house. The mansion was designed by architect Duncan Lee (also responsible for the restoration of Carters Grove in Williamsburg) and built in 1937 by Edmund Ruffin's great grandson, John Augustine Ruffin, Jr., and his wife, Mary Ball Saunders. Evelynton is listed on the National Register of Historic Places.

Shirley Plantation, the oldest plantation in Virginia, stands not far from Evelynton. Founded in 1613, only a few years after the first permanent English settlement in Jamestown, Shirley survived the Revolutionary War when the plantation served as a Continental Army supply post.

Among its many claims to fame, Shirley was the birthplace of Anne Hill Carter, mother of Confederate General Robert E. Lee. A converted laundry house at Shirley reportedly served as a

happy. She died at age 29 without having married.

Not long after Evelyn Byrd's death, Anne Harrison of nearby Berkeley Plantation reported seeing the woman's white-clad figure standing near the gravesite. Before her death Evelyn had promised Anne, a close friend, that she would return. Apparently she kept that promise.

Other, more recent, reports of ghost sightings come from house tour guides who describe sensing the presence of Evelyn Byrd, most often on the dark wooden stairs in the mansion. Others tell of seeing a weeping woman in an upstairs window at Evelynton.

Shirley Plantation with its pineapple symbol of hospitality perched high on the roof is the oldest plantation in Virginia.

As was often the case in Colonial America, the kitchen at Shirley was located in a separate building.

schoolroom where the renowned general received part of his education. In earlier times, George Washington and Thomas Jefferson were among guests who visited at Shirley.

The plantation mansion was built during the years 1723 to 1738. Its interior features excellent examples of eighteenth century craftsmanship, especially in the exquisite hand-carved wooden panels and mantels. Visitors who take time to look closely at the old glass windowpanes in the dining room will discern initials scratched on some of them. The décor emphasizes the pineapple—a colonial hospitality symbol—not only in the hand-carved interior woodwork but also in the three and a half-foot rooftop finial that welcomes guests.

Besides possessing a fascinating array of portraits, antique furniture and old family heirloom silver, Shirley Plantation features an amazing hanging

staircase that has no visible means of support. Fashioned of walnut, the stairs extend to the third floor.

Tour guides at Shirley often are willing to share a ghost story or two. A favorite tale is about an old family portrait stored for years in the attic. Occupants of the house would hear sounds of a chair rocking over their heads, but when they investigated the attic would find nothing except the portrait lying in the dust. Eventually, when the painting of Martha Hill (sister of Edward Hill who built Shirley Plantation in 1723) was moved and hung in a downstairs room, the rocking ceased.

Berkeley, site of the first Thanksgiving celebration in America, probably is best known of the James River Plantations. It served as headquarters for Union General George McClellan following the Seven Days Battle that left Evelynton in ruins. McClellan used the cellar to imprison captured members of the Confederate Army. During the Union's occupation, "Taps," the tune played at military funerals, was composed on the lawn at Berkeley.

Benjamin Harrison, signer of the Declaration of Independence, and his son, William Henry "Tippecanoe" Harrison, 23rd president of the United States, were both born at Berkeley. George Washington and the nine men who followed him as president all dined with the Harrisons at the plantation.

An abundance of lush greenery provides a shield of privacy for Berkeley Plantation. Site of the first Thanksgiving celebration and a Civil War occupation, Berkeley is one of the most famous plantations on the James River.

The lovely old house has seen its bit of tragedy. In 1744 during a severe storm, Benjamin Harrison IV, along with two of his daughters, was struck by lightning. All three died. Harrison had been attempting to lower a window in an upstairs bedroom. Since that time, tales have been told of that same window slowly closing by itself.

Besides the absolute presence of history, visitors to Berkeley are struck by the lush richness of the grounds, 10 acres of which form terraced boxwood gardens that lead from the front door to the edge of the James River. The early Georgian mansion, built in 1726, is believed to be the oldest three-story brick home in Virginia. Bricks used in Berkeley's construction were fired on the plantation grounds.

Strolling the lawns of Berkley Plantation visitors gain a sense of what it was like to live in colonial America. People who thrill to ghostly tales as well as those with a spirited sense of history will enjoy taking a side trip to the old Virginia plantations that rise in stately grandeur along the James River between Williamsburg and Richmond.

Coach House Tavern ~ A Dining Delight

*W*ant something different for dinner? Try the Coach House Tavern at Berkeley Plantation. Built partly on the original foundation of the old coach house, the restaurant has been open for more than 20 years. Staff members wearing colonial costumes serve both lunch and dinner in the tavern.

Among the delectable and unusual luncheon menu offerings, the Harrison Landing chicken salad is a favorite. Served in a fresh pineapple shell, a huge mound of chicken salad is artistically decorated with fruit, toasted almonds and a delicious serving of a tavern specialty, sweet potato salad. A wide array of croissant sandwiches, including Virginia baked ham and cheddar and Chesapeake seafood melt, are among the features.

The dinner menu includes pan-fried, pecan-crusted catfish fillet as well as venison, antelope, and a variety of unique seafood dishes. Dinner is by reservation only.

Dining in the Coach House Tavern on Berkeley Plantation allows a delightful change of pace for tourists and residents who enjoy food served with a Colonial flair.

Hilltop House, 20 by 26 inches, original pastel by Mary Montague Sikes.

MARY MONTAGUE SIKES

Blending History with the Present ~ Hilltop House Hotel

Situated on a mountaintop overlooking Harpers Ferry, West Virginia, Hilltop House, more than a century old, is a hotel that invites its guests to discover the area's historic past. Inside the structure, aged staircases ascend to floors above and hallways meander into the shadows. Outside the stone and wooden edifice, a mist rises above the confluence of the Potomac and Shenandoah Rivers. Looking down into the haze enhances the exotic view that Thomas Jefferson claimed was "worth a voyage across the Atlantic."

As visitors climb the winding stairs or wander through the hallways, they may sense visions from the past hiding in the shadows. Perhaps the ghost of one of John Brown's raiding party members lurks in the ancient hallway; perhaps it is the ghost of John Brown himself who was captured and hanged at Harpers Ferry in 1859. According to history, Brown, a leader for the abolition of slavery, led a party of 21 men in a raid to capture the federal arsenal at the strategic position of Harpers Ferry. It is said that after the capture he intended to incite area slaves into open rebellion.

For a few hours in October, 1859, Brown held hostage a group of prominent local citizens, including Col. Lewis Washington, a nephew of George Washington. Thirty-six hours later, the raid ended with the capture and wounding of Brown by U. S. Marines led by Col. Robert E. Lee. Years later, a Hollywood movie about John Brown's raid was filmed at Harpers Ferry.

Antique furnishings decorate the dining rooms and conference facilities at Hilltop House. Through the broad glass panels that shield the hotel's porches from harsh winter winds, the Shenandoah and the Potomac Rivers are visible far below. In the distance, a railroad trestle bridge is part of the daytime landscape while trains passing through add familiar sounds to the night.

In 1887, Hilltop House was built on a bluff that offers a spectacular view of three states—West Virginia, Maryland, and Virginia. At the time of the

Hilltop House Hotel

Scenic mountain views from Hilltop House add to the charm.

hotel's construction, Harpers Ferry still had not recovered from the Civil War. Both the Confederate and the Union armies had fought for control of the town—a location George Washington in his time had considered so vital. By the end of the war, the little town had changed hands more than 23 times.

Robert Harper, an architect, founded Harpers Ferry in 1747 when he started a ferry service over the Potomac and Shenandoah Rivers. By order of George Washington, a federal armory was built and began operation there in 1801. An adjacent rifle works manufactured the nation's first guns with interchangeable parts. The passing of major railroad lines through Harpers Ferry provided needed transportation and made the town into a small industrial community.

However, devastated by the war and the victim of major floods that occurred in 1870 and 1879, Harpers Ferry failed to regain its original economic potential. In recent years, the area's beauty, charm, and history have helped revitalize it into a thriving tourist attraction.

Over the years, because of the quiet splendor of its location, the hotel became a favorite retreat for

such historical figures as President Woodrow Wilson, writer Mark Twain, and inventor Alexander Graham Bell. More recently, President Bill Clinton and Vice President Al Gore have been among its guests.

Carl Sandberg immortalized the hotel in his poem, "Landscape Including Three States of the Union." Describing Harpers Ferry, he wrote, "On the main street the houses huddle: the walls crouch for cover. And yet—up at Hilltop House or up at Jefferson's Rock, there are lookouts."

During the 1950s, in order to cope with changing times Hilltop House was transformed into a center for theater, with its own theatrical group, the Hilltop Players. Hollywood stars came to join with the local theater group in some of its productions.

These days, Hilltop House is hosting "murder mystery parties." Hotel guests witness a staged murder and attempt to solve the crime. Along with prizes for the winning crime-solvers, elegant Friday, Saturday, and Sunday buffets are part of the murder mystery party package.

The hotel now has 62 air-conditioned guest rooms and suites, a restaurant that seats 340 people, and banquet facilities. Visitors are drawn to the hotel's location near mapped mountain trails for hiking, Civil War battlefields, and nearby Charles Town Racetrack.

Today enthusiastic Civil War re-enactors have helped make Harpers Ferry a major tourist attraction. Taking a short walk from Hilltop House, hotel guests discover renovated wooden and stone structures that line pleasant village streets, transforming the streets into a living reminder of the past. By entering the Wax Museum, a more than 150-year-old building on High Street, visitors interested in history relive the infamous story of John Brown, depicted through life-size figures. The small brick firehouse where Brown and his party took refuge still stands on High Street.

From Hilltop House, 250 feet above the rivers, guests often gaze across the mysterious terrain where the three states converge. Because so much blood was shed on its grounds, even on a clear day Civil War memories hang heavy in the streets of nearby Harpers Ferry. Cries of the dead and wounded echo from the past.

As hotel brochures say, "Robert Harper's Ferry is an island in the stream of time; Hilltop House is the bridge to its yesterdays."

View from Hilltop House

Harpers Ferry, a quaint village that attracts visitors year round.

The Homestead, 26 by 20 inches, original pastel by Mary Montague Sikes.

Homestead ~ Dignity and Excellence

In quiet solitude, the stately red brick tower of The Homestead rises through an early morning mist in Hot Springs. Set against lush Virginia pines, cedars, and deciduous trees heavy with fresh new leaves of spring, the Grande Dame of the Mountains appears both majestic and massive.

Nearby, at the hotel's front entrance, guests stroll in and out, passing across a long, wide veranda. Occasionally, a buggy drawn by a pair of Appaloosa horses pulls into the circular drive, ready to offer guests a scenic ride along one of the resort's well-maintained mountain trails.

Later in the day groups of people assemble inside The Homestead lobby where they enjoy afternoon tea. Seated on comfortable upholstered chairs and sofas, guests savor scones and strawberry jam delivered by efficient, uniformed waiters. Fronting tall, stately columns, the furniture edges the long, lush carpet of the Great Hall. The arrangements of tables, chairs, and sofas replicate photographs taken during the early 1900s that are displayed in the hotel.

The ambiance and activity of today's Homestead would make Captain Thomas Bullett—who built the first Homestead as a rustic wooden lodge for 15 guests—proud. His structure, completed in 1766, was named The Homestead probably in honor of the homesteaders who helped build it. Perhaps Bullett built the lodge in response to many requests from visitors to the springs for room and board in his home.

A bathhouse in the form of an octagonal building was constructed at Warm Springs even earlier, opening in 1761. That building, claimed to be the "oldest spa building in America," was erected around the warm springs pool. The large white structure remains intact today and is much as it was when first built. It surrounds an octagonal pool that contains 40,000 gallons of clear flowing mineral spring water. The Jefferson Pools, named in honor of the man who helped make them famous, remain a part of The Homestead facilities. Hotel guests are ferried there daily to enjoy the waters.

Scenic Bath County, site of The Homestead, claims a rich history. Legend has it that in the early 1600s an American Indian discovered the warm

1766, the year of the establishment of the Hot Springs baths, is designated with flowers and greenery by the front driveway of the Homestead.

mineral springs reflecting the light of evening stars. After falling asleep in the shallow springs, he awakened empowered with new stamina and mental abilities. Following this experience, according to the legend, the brave took only two days to run through the mountains to the site of an important tribal conference near the coast. There he told of his discovery, and because of his new wisdom and speaking eloquence he was elected to lead the tribes. Panel number one in the Jefferson Parlor at The Homestead depicts the legend of that Indian brave.

Traveling along old buffalo trails, colonial explorers and surveyors started coming to the Hot Springs area in the early 1700s. By the 1750s, homesteaders, lured by the mild climate and scenic vistas, had built cabins around many of the springs. George Washington was one of the early trekkers over the rough trails through the mountain gaps as he traveled to inspect forts along the Jackson River.

Thomas Jefferson was another famous visitor who came seeking relief from "rheumatism" in the warm soothing waters of the springs. A guest ledger from Warm Springs Hotel, now in The Homestead archives, documents a visit by Jefferson in 1818. During his three-week visit, he took the waters twice a day and also visited The Homestead at least once during his stay.

An octagonal room known as the Jefferson Parlor, opening off the lobby, gives tribute to Jefferson's interest in The Homestead. Each panel on the wall features a painting, beginning with the Indian legend about the discovery of Hot Springs. Jefferson Pools at Warm Spring are depicted in the next panel; then another painting shows Thomas Jefferson overlooking Hot Springs. America's first mineral bath spa is shown in the next panel.

Other panels illustrate Dr. Goode's Hotel at Hot Springs in 1832, Healing Springs that served as a Confederate hospital, Cascades Gorge, and impressive Falling Springs. The C & O Railroad bringing guests to The Homestead is depicted as is the 1901 fire that destroyed the hotel. Another painted panel shows the tower that was completed in 1929 and which now symbolizes The Homestead. The last panel illustrates the Flag Rock at the pinnacle of Warm Springs Mountain. All of the panels were painted on site by Virginia artist Lee Baskerville.

Dr. Goode is said to have been The Homestead's first real developer. From a prominent Virginia family, the physician was well traveled and, from his journeys,

brought back a new spa treatment, that of hydrotherapy—the Spout Bath. The treatment consists of directing warm mineral springs water in a pressurized stream directly onto the ailing parts of a human body. Waters flowing at a constant temperature of 105 degrees Fahrenheit came directly from the Spout Spring through pipes formed by hollowing out trunks of chestnut trees.

A successful marketer, Dr. Goode enlarged the hotel and added more dining and kitchen facilities. He also built a beautiful ballroom that helped establish The Homestead's reputation as a place to come for romance and courtship. Not only could young people go on horseback and carriage rides but they could also attend dances and balls.

During Dr. Goode's ownership, as many as 6,000 visitors a year flocked to the resort. Drawn by promises of the curative powers of the springs water, travelers from the northeast endured a four-day journey that included a two-day stagecoach ride over terrible rutted mountain roads.

In 1858, Dr. Goode died. In the following years,

The Homestead tower is a Hot Springs landmark.

Homestead guests enjoy the mountain air from rockers on the hotel's front porch.

The Homestead had a number of absentee owners. During the Civil War, soldiers from both armies probably stayed in the hotel as they crossed through the valley. War virtually eliminated public travel, so few visitors came to the spa. After the war, General and Mrs. Robert E. Lee enjoyed the benefits of the mineral springs and influenced others to visit The Homestead.

The Homestead experienced growth once more after a corporation that included banker J. Pierpont Morgan and C & O Railroad president Melville Ingalls bought the facility in 1888. Railroad tracks were laid from Covington and rail service began in the valley in 1892. That same year, most of the buildings on The Homestead grounds were razed and a new hotel was built. As an impressive addition, a new Homestead Spa with luxurious private massage and hydrotherapy rooms was constructed.

For a resort that for so many years was located on the edge of the wilderness territory, the installation of The Homestead's first generator in 1892 enabled a major step into a new era. During the same period, miles of trails, drives, and walkways were built. A new West Wing addition enhanced the hotel, and the grounds were landscaped to include a six-hole golf course and some tennis courts. The Casino, now a tennis and golf-pro shop, and a stone bathhouse were also built.

Afternoon tea is served to guests in the well-furnished Great Hall of the Homestead.

During the Independence Day holiday of 1901 a catastrophic fire destroyed the resort. After only three hours, all that remained were charred brick chimneys and thick smoke. However, quick work by hotel staff saved the Spa building. Demolishing the walkway that connected the hotel's West Wing to the Spa, they were able to prevent the Spa from catching fire. The Spa building stands today as the most historic on the property.

Within a few days of the disaster, gifted architects were on site making plans for a new Homestead. Since the fire occurred at a time when modern insurance was unheard of, the resort was fortunate to have had the support of J. Pierpont Morgan. A new hotel, built of red brick, limestone, and steel, rose from the ashes of the old and opened on March 10, 1902. The West Wing opened in 1904, the East Wing in 1914, and the Tower opened to considerable fanfare in 1929. Designed by New York architect Charles Delavan Wetmore, the Tower today stands as the single most recognizable feature of The Homestead resort.

Joey Keyes and his Appaloosas, Popcorn and Cheyenne, take guests for carriage rides around the golf courses or along the Cascade trails.

A well-lighted stained glass window is part of the décor in the wine room at the Homestead.

Completion of the Tower addition came at an unfortunate time because of the country's financial collapse and the great depression that followed. Since many of the guests who normally frequented the resort were struck by financial loss, hotel bookings were down. The new addition was not adequately financed and by 1938 the parent Virginia Hot Springs Company was forced into bankruptcy. Fortunately, The Homestead survived reorganization under bankruptcy courts. It also withstood a brief four-month closure during World War II when it served as a secure internment location for several hundred Japanese diplomats and their families.

During the war, The Homestead was the site of an important international event—the United Nations Conference on Food and Agriculture. This was said to be a trial run for the United Nations, and it proved a great success.

In the years following the war, The Homestead deteriorated. The age of the once grand lady showed especially in the Spa. Long-time loyal patrons and through Hot Springs during 1756—ten years before The Homestead was actually built.

Other presidential portraits include those of Thomas Jefferson, William McKinley, William Howard Taft, Woodrow Wilson, Calvin Coolidge, Herbert Hoover, Franklin D. Roosevelt, Harry S. Truman, Dwight Eisenhower, Lyndon B. Johnson, Richard M. Nixon, Gerald R. Ford, James E. Carter, Ronald Reagan, and William J. Clinton. Many of these men visited prior to becoming president, when they were governors of their states or in Congress. They are by artist Paul Bertholet.

Since its early years, tradition and relaxation have been hallmarks of The Homestead. Afternoon tea in the Great Hall continues. So do the easy relaxation of scenic carriage rides, the pleasure of golf events, tennis matches, walks in the warm Virginia sunshine, bowling, horseback rides, or dining in evening elegance in one of a choice of dining rooms.

The Homestead once again stands as the grand lady of the Virginia Mountains. Guests glory in horseback or carriage rides along its scenic trails as they create new and unforgettable memories of a special hotel.

Vibrant gardens of colorful flowers brighten the exterior of the world-renowned Spa building at the Homestead.

the staff worried the declining resort would close or be bought up by a hotel chain.

Matters came to a pleasant resolution in 1993 when ClubCorp Resorts purchased the property, and under the leadership of Robert Dedman and his son, Bob, The Homestead has returned to its days of earlier glory. The more than 500 rooms and the parlors and suites have undergone or are undergoing restoration. Millions of dollars have been spent to refurbish guestrooms, restore the Spa, improve The Old Course and the tennis courts, and renovate The Great Hall, The Casino, and The Dining Room. As in the past, guests feel special and secure knowing they will be able to return and find The Homestead as they left it—elegant and dignified.

They can find a table in the President's Lounge and look out over a panoramic view of a golf course and meadow that flank The Homestead. Along the walls, portraits of 16 American presidents who have visited the resort stare out at guests. These include George Washington who was believed to have gone

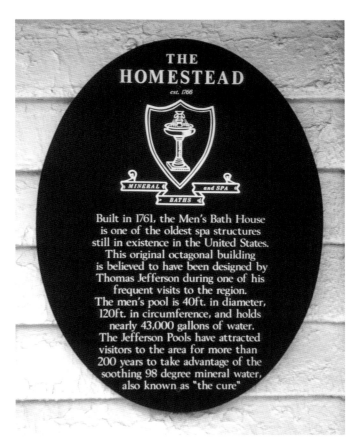

Plaque at Jefferson Pools

The spacious indoor pool in the Homestead Spa, naturally heated with spring-fed water.

The Homestead owns the Jefferson Pools, located at Warm Springs. Established in 1761, reportedly the oldest spa building in America, it features an octagonal gentleman's pool.

Long-time Staff Member Welcomes Back Guests

For more than 44 years, Woodrow "Woodie" Pettus has welcomed guests returning to The Homestead. Standing at the entrance to the main dining room, Woodie smiles and says, "I still love what I'm doing."

From the enthusiasm he displays as he greets friends, young and old, he obviously enjoys coming to work each day and would not wish to trade in his very special job. A Bath County native, Woodie explains that his father worked at The Homestead and now his son is assistant banquet manager for the resort.

"It's been great," he says. "We've had a good time, and I'm happy things are at top level again."

Reliable, caring employees such as Woodie and his family have helped The Homestead maintain a loyal following of return guests over the years. "Our people are what makes this place," says Mary Sanders, Director of Marketing. "It would be hard to replace some of these people."

Glancing across the President's Lounge, Sanders waves a greeting to a returning guest. "You feel like you are visiting a part of a family," she says. "You leave feeling cared for. Guests who return year after year think of us as friends."

"There are so many who have been here for generations—mother and grandmother," John Hoover, The Homestead historian, explains.

"There's a sense of ownership by staff," Sanders points out. "They are very sincere, wanting you to feel welcome."

Many members of the dining staff are from Jamaica. As long ago as 1905, The Homestead began bringing up staff members from the islands. The population of Bath County is not large enough to meet all of the resort's staffing requirements, Hoover says.

"Many of the Jamaicans who come here today work on luxury cruise ships part of the year," Hoover points out.

"Jamaicans are taught from early on to be gracious and to provide proper formal service," Sanders says. "Many come back every year for 15 or 20 years."

The Homestead is a popular year-round destination. The resort now employs more than 1,000 people and offers employee housing and recreational facilities.

"It's important to have a high ratio of employees to guests to maintain our standards," Hoover explains.

"The Homestead has been known since the 1800s for its meeting facilities," Sanders says. "The Virginia Bar Association has met here every year for over 100 years."

The Southern Surgical Society has held its meetings at The Homestead every other year for more than 100 years.

Thomas Edison and Henry Ford were among the many great minds who have met at The Homestead. "For many years they came with their families," Hoover points out. "They loved to walk and talk … Guests today love to walk the same trails."

Guests also take comfort in returning to find old friends like Woody still around, ready to make certain they will enjoy their stay. It is a special kind of Homestead hospitality that spans more than 234 years of making guests feel they have "a home away from home."

The European-style Spa, recently restored, is kept in immaculate condition. Seven springs are on the Homestead property. Two are hot at 105 degrees, two are warm at 98 degrees, and three are cold. They are still piped into the Spa.

The Cascades Gorge, fed by its own set of springs, is owned by The Homestead. Thomas Edison, who provided the Homestead's first three generators, and Henry Ford, another frequent guest, enjoyed walking and talking with each other along the Cascades' trails.

Keswick Hall, 20 by 26 inches, original pastel by Mary Montague Sikes.

Keswick Hall at Monticello

Keswick Hall at Monticello, glowing with a sense of place and history, rises like a pale yellow jewel from a lush green meadow. Set deep in Virginia horse country, not far from the historic city of Charlottesville, the resort sits atop land that Thomas Jefferson considered his Utopia. Monticello, the magnificent home Jefferson spent much of his life designing and building, is only minutes away.

Years ago a pre-Civil War mansion named Broad Oak was built on the Keswick Estate and remained on the property until the late 1800s. Villa Crawford, now part of the expanded Keswick Hall resort, was built on the estate in 1912. A Georgian-style building with white stucco over tile, the house originally cost more than $100,000 and featured a 35 by 40-foot reception hall, 17 other rooms, and a large number of bathrooms.

In 1947, a Charlottesville realtor, Donald G. Stevens, led a group to purchase Villa Crawford and transform it and neighboring property into a 527-acre country club featuring golf and tennis. The villa, now the clubhouse, features dining rooms, lounges, and guestrooms for members.

Stevens was enthusiastic about the club's potential because 20 years earlier he had led a group that purchased the Warner Wood estate. He used the Jefferson-designed manor house as a centerpiece for creating Farmington Country Club. Because the Farmington property had gained a world-renowned reputation, Stevens expected Keswick Country Club to do equally well.

But it did not. The club lacked the support of the community and after 10 years was a financial failure.

Today, Keswick Hall at Monticello is everything Stevens had hoped for. The change began after Sir Bernard Ashley purchased the property. In 1991 the villa was expanded into what is now an impressive resort. The original mansion, complete with heart pine floors and grand staircases, became the north wing of Keswick Hall. The seventeen guestrooms are all decorated with Laura Ashley wallpaper and fabric.

Each guestroom has its own theme and color scheme. A returning guest might wish to request the tennis room or the room with the airplane theme. Other theme rooms include fishing, maps, the circus, and music. Old prints, books, porcelain, and even old family photographs are part of each room's décor.

Some rooms open onto their own balconies.

The Italian Renaissance-style Keswick Hall stands on a green hillside at the edge of Virginia's Blue Ridge Mountains

Others share terraces with up to five other rooms. Some have canopy beds and armoires so large they have to be taken apart to be moved.

Keswick's elevators have one unforgettable element—seven original oil-painted panels that line the walls. The wooden floor in the original section of the hotel provides a major distinction between the villa and the addition that is carpeted.

In all there are 47 guestrooms and one suite. More than 8000 square feet of meeting and conference space are available on the property and can accommodate gatherings as small as eight and or as large as 400, About 40 percent of the Keswick Hall's business comes from the conference market. Some "high end" corporations like to set their board meetings at this upscale location.

At least twice and often as many as four times a year, the entire resort is booked for a lavish weekend wedding. To house the reception, a spacious white tent is sometimes set up on the lawn adjacent to the North Wing.

Keswick Country Club is on the property and available for use by guests. The grounds feature an Olympic 25-meter lap pool, an indoor/outdoor pool, and three clay and two hard tennis courts, as well as

The Keswick Hall shield hangs above a mantel in the lobby.

fitness equipment. The resort also offers an 18-hole Arnold Palmer-designed golf course where golfers can enjoy the scenic countryside. A number of dining options includes the Ashley Room, open for dinner on certain days. Besides using European recipes, the chef features "the best of modern American cuisine."

Keswick Club, a paneled dining room in the clubhouse decorated with a variety of golf clubs, serves up to 50 people at a time for lunch and some dinners. Favorite foods include the cheese biscuits and the big "21" Burger. Golf-view terraces are open for casual lunch, and the Pavilion, by the pool, offers light luncheon fare.

The gift shop in the clubhouse has a Hunt Club flavor. As well as an array of riding and other sports clothing, the shop is decorated with hunting prints and offers for sale a history of the Keswick Hunt Club.

Situated within a 600-acre gated community, Keswick Hall is six miles from Charlottesville and four miles from Monticello and the Michie Tavern. More than 10 Virginia wineries are within easy driving and well worth the visit.

In addition to accommodations and a three-course dinner, one hotel package includes passes to Monticello, Ash Lawn, Highland and Michie Taverns, and a Jefferson cup. It's a tribute to Thomas Jefferson's love for his Virginia paradise.

"Preferred Hotels & Resorts World Wide" and "Orient-Express" brass emblems hang at the entrance of Keswick Hall.

Thomas Jefferson's Monticello

Probably no other home in America is as fascinating as Thomas Jefferson's Monticello. It was Jefferson—author of the Declaration of Independence, founder of the University of Virginia, and third president of the United States—who sent Lewis and Clark to explore the West.

Monticello, built over a period of 40 years, the only house in America to be on the United Nations' World Heritage List of international treasurers, is Jefferson's biography etched in brick, glass and mortar.

Inspired by the Virginia landscape where he was born, Jefferson chose the top of an 867-foot wooded mountain as the site of his dream plantation, Monticello—little mountain. These woods, where young Jefferson played as a child, are part of the land he inherited from his father when he was only 14 years old.

In 1768 Jefferson leveled the land on the top of his mountain and began building Monticello. Constructing a home on a mountain was highly unusual during colonial times, a period when, because of transportation concerns, most houses were erected along the chief highway system of the time—the rivers, lakes, and oceans.

Jefferson used his own trees for the source of timber for Monticello. The building's foundation was created from stone blocks cut from the mountain, and a kiln was built on the mountaintop to fire the bricks. The hardware for doors and window glass came from England.

By 1770 the South Pavilion was finished and—since Shadwell, Jefferson's birthplace, had burned earlier—he moved to the mountain. The two-story main house, including a double-decked portico modeled after Andrea Palladio's Villa Pisani, was completed in 1774.

During the five years Jefferson spent as the U. S. minister to France, his ideas about architecture changed. After visiting and studying European gardens and buildings, he realized that, unlike city

This view of the Blue Ridge Mountains led Thomas Jefferson to build his famous Monticello home.

buildings, tall structures were unnecessary on the vast and rolling Virginia landscape. He returned to Monticello determined to redesign his Utopian house into a "modern country home."

Among the renovations Jefferson began in 1796 were the removal of the upper portico and the addition of a dome to the center of Monticello. The first glass-domed dwelling seen in America, the center section was used during Jefferson's time as the children's playroom. In 1797, Jefferson obtained the services of James Dinmore, a Philadelphia house builder, for the remodeling project that would continue on until 1809.

Unlike most other large colonial homes, Monticello lacks a grand staircase. Jefferson felt this would take up too much space, so to accommodate traffic to the upper floors he hid away two small stairways, each only two feet wide, in the north and south passages.

French art that Jefferson purchased was placed in the first floor parlor. His bedroom, library, and study were all in the south wing on the first floor.

In 1815 the 6000 volumes from his library were sold to the United States government and used to start the Library of Congress. Unfortunately the many years Jefferson had spent in public service, including serving as Governor of Virginia and President of the United States, led to his failure to attend to his own personal and financial affairs.

Ironically, Thomas Jefferson died on July 4, 1826, exactly 50 years after the adoption of the Declaration of Independence. In 1827, in order to pay creditors, his slaves and the majority of the furnishings in Monticello were sold.

In 1834 a Jefferson admirer, Navy Lt. Uriah P. Levy, bought Monticello and at his death willed it to the American people. However, the United States government gave up the claim and thus followed a 17-year battle among some of Levy's heirs for the property. Meanwhile, Monticello fell into disrepair because the farmer who leased it from the heirs did not keep it up.

During the Civil War, Monticello was taken over by the Confederate government. In 1879 Jefferson Monroe Levy, the nephew of Uriah Levy, took possession of the very run-down estate and tried to improve it. On April 13, 1923, on the 180th anniversary of the birth of Thomas Jefferson, the Thomas Jefferson Memorial Foundation, Inc. bought the property from Levy for $500,000.

Major restoration began in 1938, and in 1940 the Garden Club of Virginia funded restoration of both the east and west portico gardens.

Today one can stop at the Monticello Visitors Center to view an excellent movie, *Thomas Jefferson: the Pursuit of Liberty*. The Center offers a comprehensive exhibit of archaeological artifacts and personal belongings of Jefferson. This includes diagrams and architectural displays detailing the many changes that took place at Monticello over the years.

Notable on the Monticello grounds is Mulberry Row, the central building site for the plantation. According to a brochure, in 1796, "there were seventeen buildings, including a stable, joinery, blacksmith shop, nailery, utility sheds, and dwellings for the slave and free labor force." Only a workman's cottage, part of a stable, and ruins of the joinery remain today along the plantation road that once was so filled with activity.

In 1773 Jefferson himself laid out the graveyard where he is buried. The obelisk above his grave inscribes his words: "Here was buried Thomas Jefferson, Author of the Declaration of American Independence, of the Statute of Virginia for Religious Freedom, and Father of the University of Virginia."

Michie Tavern and Meadow Run Grist Mill

Michie Tavern, near Keswick Hall, is a Virginia
Historic Landmark built about 1784.

M ichie Tavern is a Virginia Historic Landmark built in about 1784. Established by a Scotsman, William Michie, the tavern was a community social center and a place of lodging as well as food and drink for travelers.

Moved 17 miles in 1927, Michie Tavern is now located close to Monticello. An example of Colonial Revival buildings, the tavern is open to visitors for a midday meal that comes complete with costumed servers.

The nearby Meadow Run Grist Mill, built about 1797, is now used as a General Store. A detailed description of the operation of a grist mill is given on audiotape in a room beneath the store where equipment is displayed.

*European garden flowers decorate the courtyard and
other entrances to Keswick Hall.*

Meadow Run Grist Mill, built about 1797, is now used as a General Store.

Operation of the mill is explained in an audiotape played in the equipment room beneath the store.

Hotel du Pont ~ *Wilmington, Delaware*

Hotel du Pont, 20 by 26 inches, original pastel by Mary Montague Sikes.

Exploring the Hotel du Pont

An atmosphere of warmth fills the lobby of the Hotel du Pont and radiates throughout the luxurious hotel facility. Opened in 1913, the hotel is uniquely located in the corporate headquarters building of the DuPont Company and is owned by the company. It is said to be the "premier business and corporate meeting establishment in Delaware."

Originally built to give the city of Wilmington one of the most attractive and comfortable hotels of its time, Hotel du Pont has undergone renovations and changes over the years that have assured its continued importance to the center of the city.

The hotel opened January 15, 1913, the birthday of Pierre S. du Pont, president of Hotel Du Pont Company. A detailed description of that opening day is contained in a book by Harry V. Ayres, *Hotel du Pont Story*, published in 1981. Ayres was the hotel's sixth manager and served in that capacity for 10 years.

In his book he describes the Hotel du Pont as "a picture window through which the public may look at the character of the company." One third of the building is devoted to the hotel, the other two-thirds to company headquarters.

The chosen location at the corner of 11th and Market Streets in Wilmington was important to the hotel's success. The hill on which it stands overlooks the Brandywine, Christina, and Delaware rivers. Today the hotel faces Rodney Square.

Ayres' book describes activities of the first week, citing that 25,000 visitors toured the white stone Italian Renaissance building. On opening day, he wrote, lines began to form at 8 a.m. as visitors awaited the opportunity to explore the hotel's elaborate lobby, dining rooms, and ballroom.

It took two and a half years for French and Italian craftsmen to carve, paint, and gild the lavish interior of the 20-story hotel. The polished wood paneling, Queen Anne and Chippendale furniture, high ceilings, and gleaming marble remain today, giving the Hotel du Pont its distinctive individuality.

Not long after the hotel opened, management received a number of requests from people who

Hotel du Pont lobby features an original decorative ceiling. A full range of celebrities has passed through this lobby, including such notables as Charles A. Lindbergh, Amelia Earhart, General Douglas MacArthur, Prince Rainier, and a multitude of Hollywood actors and actresses.

wanted to take up permanent residence in the hotel. Pierre S. du Pont used four or five of the hotel's rooms, and other wealthy elderly citizens rented suites, choosing to not continue maintaining their large homes. As time went on, problems arose from residents who refused to have their rooms inspected.

Ayres wrote that some fed pigeons from their room windows, and that one permanent guest actually left a window open while he was away, allowing a pigeon to come inside and build a nest. Some permanent residents moved from the du Pont after the sudden stock market slide of 1929 and The Great Depression adversely affected their fortunes. Eventually a policy was set to no longer accept permanent guests.

During World War II, a group of U.S. Air Force pilots, including then Captain Barry Goldwater, were quartered in the Hotel du Pont for the period of time when they were flying aircraft from New Castle Airport to bases overseas.

Carolyn Grubb, Public Relations Manager, has been with the Hotel du Pont for 25 years and assisted

Chandeliers and mirrors help create the elegant beauty of the Gold Ballroom.

Ayres with his book. She says the hotel is unique in the hospitality industry because most of the management staff has been with it for 15 years or more.

"The employees become part of the fabric of the hotel," Grubb says. "They can walk into a beautiful lobby…. The people make it successful. That's why we have so many people coming back."

The hotel's Gold Ballroom is perhaps its most memorable room. Designed by Raymond M. Hood and built in 1918, five years after the du Pont first opened, the ballroom features a 27-foot ceiling. Bas-relief medallions created by Violet Terwilliger extol 20 women well known for their deeds in history, including the Indian maiden Pocahontas, Catherine the Great of Russia, Empress Josephine, and the Queen of Sheba.

Classical scenes by Duncan Smith, executed by Italian artisans, decorate the walls of the Gold Ballroom. The floor-to-ceiling murals were created with the sgraffito process that involves the application of five different colored layers of plaster. Artisans carved the plaster to a variety of depths to expose the different colors. A topcoat was then added to provide more details.

Gold leaf balconies overlook the Gold Ballroom. The du Barry Room originally opened onto the balconies, but safety concerns in recent years required the blocking off of those doorways.

Two large hand-carved chandeliers hang from the French neoclassic ceiling, sending reflected bits of light to the polished oak floor. Corinthian columns frame the wide slanted mirrors on the walls of the ballroom. The arched windows are covered with luxurious gold draperies.

The ballroom is dedicated to love, Grubb is quick to assert. That's why so many wedding receptions are held there, making it necessary to book the events two years in advance. Cartouches are located over the doors at the corners of the room. The figures humorously portray courtship of fishes, stars, and birds.

An elaborate roseal marble stairway with a polished steel and bronze balustrade leads up to the du Barry Room above the ballroom. Smaller but equally as elegant as the ballroom, the du Barry features a crystal chandelier from Yugoslavia and shiny parquet floors. Twelve-foot high walnut doors carved with peacock relief sculptures lead into the room.

Until several years ago the room's mirrored doors opened onto balconies that overlooked the Gold Ballroom. Safety concerns led to their closure, and visitors must now stand below on the ballroom floor to see the ornate balconies that once teemed with romance.

In 1988 the King and Queen of Sweden stayed at the Hotel du Pont and used the Gold Ballroom to celebrate the 350th anniversary of the first landing of Swedes in America. The entourage of 100, plus 50 secret service agents, required 150 rooms to accommodate them for the night.

Dining has always been significant at the Hotel du Pont. The Green Room's Sunday brunch that first started more than 50 years ago continues in popularity and now attracts the children and grandchildren of its first dining guests. With jazz music accompaniment, the brunch features an appetizer buffet with several unusual offerings, including spinach salad mimosa with warm bacon dressing and zucchini nut bread. Entrees include Black Forest eggs

The Gold Ballroom is dedicated to love. The courtship of doves, cupids, and fish are depicted in cartouches over doors at each corner. Love and romance is portrayed in an octagonal plaque.

benedict and stuffed capon breast. Children 12 and under dine for less than half price, and those five and under eat free.

Elegance fills every niche of the Green Room, including the charming entrance foyer with its Italian mosaic floor hidden from view for many years by carpets. Three impressive original oil paintings hang in ornate frames on the fumed oak paneled walls of the dining room. Tall expansive windows look out over both Market and 11th Streets. Huge 24-carat gold-plated chandeliers weighing 2,500 pounds each hang from the oak-beam coffered ceiling.

The dark-paneled Brandywine Room and adjoining Christina Room offer a more intimate dining experience. The walls of both rooms are crowded with pieces from the du Pont's valuable 700-plus painting collection. Much of the artwork in these two rooms is by members of the Wyeth family—N.C., Andrew, and Jamie.

One painting is by another family member, Andrew N. Wyeth, son of Nathaniel Wyeth, a DuPont chemist. Nathaniel created the paint colors used in "Island Funeral," the painting by N.C. Wyeth that hangs over the fireplace in the Christina Room.

Another interesting feature of the Brandywine and Christina Rooms is the secret door into the adjacent theater. According to Henry Dawson, Brandywine Room manager, as the curtain went up and the play began, it was the practice of some of the men to slip out of the theater through the door into the hotel bar where they conducted business. Five minutes before the end, a bell rang in the bar signaling the men it was time to return to the play.

The Brandywine Room menu includes a variety of gourmet main courses, such as striped bass with macadamian nut crust, grilled marinated yellow-fin tuna, and shiitake crusted chicken breast. Milk chocolate strawberry layer cake is only one of many delicious dessert offerings.

For more informal dining, there is the Lobby Lounge with a baby grand piano where live entertainment is provided during the early evening. Small tables and Queen Anne-style chairs fill much of the room for use by diners when luncheon buffets and cocktails and hors d'oeuvres are served.

In his book about the hotel, Ayres wrote extensively regarding the loyalty of dining staff members. "The average length of employment for waitresses and their assistants is over twenty-five years," he said.

Ellen Webster, Chef Concierge, has been with the hotel for more than 25 years. She enjoys getting to meet actresses and actors who stay at the du Pont while performing in the Playhouse Theatre (part of

Elegant curving roseal marble stairways with polished steel and bronze balustrades lead to the du Barry Room in the Hotel du Pont.

the hotel building.)

"I get to meet CEOs from corporations all over the world…. I know people from all over the world because I've worked here so long," she confides with a smile.

The King and Queen of Sweden made a special impression on Webster. "It was such an incredible experience," she recalls. So much so that she named her Labrador retriever for King Carl Gustaf.

During a time when so much in the hotel industry is similar, the Hotel du Pont continues to have its own personality. Although it has changed and improved with the times, the best of its décor remains as it was in the beginning—unique, elaborate, and grand. A charter member of Preferred Hotels & Resorts Worldwide and a member of Historic Hotels of America, the Hotel du Pont is a hotel most visitors are unlikely to forget.

Joseph Hardison tends the Lobby Lounge lunch buffet.

Two 12-foot high American walnut doors lead from the Hotel du Pont lobby into the Gold Ballroom suite. Set in Italian roseal marble, the doors feature hand-carved peacock and urn designs.

An attractive chandelier hangs above the Hotel du Pont lobby.

For 50 years families have come to the Hotel du Pont to enjoy Sunday brunch in the Green Room with its Italian 24-karat gold chandeliers. David Jubity, dining captain, and waitress, Leigh Ann McLoughton, stand at the Green Room entrance. For many years the exotic mosaic tile floor was covered with carpeting.

Hotel du Pont's Art Collection

*A*t the Hotel du Pont more than 700 works of original art make up the impressive collection on display, not only in public areas but in guestrooms as well. This is said to be one of the best and largest collections of its kind in America. In 1981, the collection was subject of a major exhibition at the Delaware Art Museum.

During the 1940s the hotel began to purchase local art for a redecoration program. Most of the watercolors in the collection came from the Clothes Line Fair, sponsored by a local art group, and from the annual Christmas Shop, held in the Gold Ballroom at the hotel. Other work came from art festivals and private showings.

Some of the most famous work in the collection is by members of the Wyeth family, including Andrew Wyeth and his father, N. C. Wyeth, well known for his textbook illustrations. Work by Andrew's son, Jamie Wyeth is also on display. Other family work is by Andrew Nathaniel Wyeth, Andrew's cousin, and Ann Wyeth McCoy, N. C.'s daughter.

The Hotel du Pont's art collection is a tribute to the Brandywine Valley region of Delaware and neighboring Pennsylvania, since most of the represented artists grew up in the area or are in some way closely connected to it. Howard Pyle, one of N.C. Wyeth's teachers, is represented in the collection. His detailed painting, "Conestoga Powder Wagon," hangs in the hotel.

The Brandywine Valley offers numerous cultural opportunities for visitors to the Hotel du Pont. The Brandywine River Museum offers one of the largest Andrew Wyeth collections in America. The Delaware History Museum runs changing exhibitions depicting historical events that took place in the state, which is one of the original 13 colonies.

Fort Christina is the site of the first landing of settlers in Delaware in 1638. Elutherian Mills, the first du Pont family home, is part of the Hagley Museum that features the original powder mill and traces the history of water-powered mills. The Hagley is located on Rt. 141 in Wilmington. Nemours, a du Pont family 102-room mansion, is located in Wilmington and is open for tours.

Winterthur Museum, another du Pont mansion with 196 rooms, is known for its world's premier collection of American decorative arts. Among its many treasures are Paul Revere's silver tankards. The museum features original plasterwork, paneling, stairs, and other details from Colonial America.

With so much to see in the area, guests at the Hotel du Pont are tempted to return again and again.

Island Funeral by N. C. Wyeth. Nathaniel Wyeth, a DuPont chemist, created some of the colors used in the funeral painting that hangs over a mantel in the Brandywine Room.

Discovering the du Pont Story at Hagley Museum

To discover the origin of the DuPont Company, one needs to visit the Hagley Museum in Brandywine Valley. That's where the du Pont story begins.

Set on 235 scenic acres, the Hagley Museum is a "park-like" showcase of what life was like for workers and their families living in nineteenth century. There, visitors may roam from industrial ruins to restorations. Not only can they see how people lived, but they may view antique machinery from those days as well as a Conestoga Wagon.

The first DuPont product was gunpowder. Today's visitors to the Hagley can watch the water-powered iron wheel as it turns to mix gunpowder ingredients. The water energy for the sixteen-ton wheel comes from the nearby Brandywine River.

Elutherian Mills, the Georgian-style home for five generations of du Ponts, highlights one of the Hagley tours. The house, built in 1803, is especially festive during the Christmas season when nineteenth century decorations adorn its rooms.

Visiting the Henry Clay Mill is part of another tour that focuses on both the history of the Brandywine Valley and that of the DuPont Company. Models, exhibits, and dioramas show the growth of industrialization in America. The powder yard is on the site of the largest black powder works in the country during the mid-nineteenth century. (E. I. du Pont was the founder and also the first director.)

Those who enjoy strolling through gardens and wooded areas can walk among some of the ninety-four varieties and species of trees that spread over the acreage. The E. I. du Pont gardens, its history, and ten of the trees highlight the tour.

During Black History Month, celebrated nationally in February each year, a special program focuses on early 20th century African-American Schools. Because the state of Delaware provided little funding for those schools, Pierre S. du Pont spent $6 million to construct modern facilities for African-American children. He provided the money for the state's only free African American secondary school, Howard High School. Part of the Hagley program includes oral history presentations by some of those who attended the du Pont funded schools.

Children's tours at Hagley take them to Gibbons House, a restored foreman's home, and to Brandywine Manufacturers' Sunday School on Blacksmith Hill. Kindergartners through third graders get to dress up in period costumes and attend classes in a typical nineteenth century school. Fourth through sixth graders can spend a full day participating in nineteenth century experiences.

Arrangements to tour the Hagley Museum may be made by contacting the Wilmington Delaware office, P.O. Box 3630. The zip code is 19807-0630.

The Hagley is an educational side trip for guests at the Hotel du Pont.

The Playhouse Theatre

Known as Wilmington's Little Broadway, the Playhouse Theatre brings extra magic to a stay at the Hotel du Pont. Opened in 1913 and built in only 150 days, the Playhouse is said to be "one of the finest examples of Victorian theatre architecture."

The biggest stars of both stage and screen have appeared on the Playhouse stage, inside the Hotel du Pont building. Alice Brady, once billed as the "Queen of Movie Stars," appeared many times at the Playhouse.

The entrance hall is filled with black and white photos of famous stars who have appeared at the theater. They include: Lauren Bacall, Tyrone Power, Sir Lawrence Olivier, Carol Channing, Helen Hayes, Rosalind Russell, and many more.

Seating 1,248 people, the Playhouse was designed by New York architect Charles A. Rich, with audience comfort in mind. Seats are spaced so no one need stand to permit other theatergoers to pass by. As in other parts of the hotel building, lovely crystal chandeliers hang from the ceiling.

At the time of the theater's opening, October 15, 1913, the stage was larger than all but three New York City stages. Ticket prices ranged from 25 cents for a balcony seat to $2.50 for orchestra or box seats.

The Playhouse Theatre is the only one in the country that has operated non-stop since it opened. There has never been a dark season.

"It is sort of a pre-Broadway," says Carolyn Grubb, Hotel du Pont public relations manager.

She points out, "You can dine here, go to the theater, and you don't have to go out of the hotel."

Theater season runs from October to May. Six stage productions are offered during the season.

Carolyn Grubb, Hotel du Pont Director of Public Relations, stands in the Playhouse lobby. The very popular theatre productions are "sort of pre-Broadway," she says.

_The Playhouse Theatre, located in the Hotel du Pont building, is said to be the
only theatre in this country that has operated every season since it opened._

Built in 1913, the Playhouse Theatre is a fine example of Victorian architecture. This is a scene from the beautiful interior. A secret door in the theatre once allowed men to slip from the audience into the hotel bar where they conducted business. A bell was rung in the bar five minutes before the intermission to give the men time to get back.

Part II

Hotels of the South

Hotel Vinoy, 26 by 20 inches, original pastel by Mary Montague Sikes.

Hotel Vinoy Glistens in the Sunlight

Glistening in the sunlight, scores of yachts and sailboats rock and bob gracefully on the waters of Tampa Bay fronting the landmark Renaissance Vinoy Resort Hotel. And the marina is only a part of the Vinoy's magnificent waterfront view.

Since its restoration and reopening in the early 1990s, the Mediterranean Revival-style hotel once again has taken its place as a dominant feature on the edge of the bay. People of all ages are attracted to the impressive salmon-colored resort that stretches out in regal elegance along the sands.

Built in 1925 on land that cost $35 when purchased in the 1880s, the Vinoy, not surprisingly, is listed on the National Register of Historic Places and is a member of the Historic Hotels of America. It opened on New Year's Eve 1925 as one of the most expensive hotels in Florida, charging $20 per night including meals.

As in the early days of the Vinoy Park Hotel, celebrities—including presidents, governors, tennis players, and movie stars—often are still seen lingering in the lobby. The stenciled pecky cypress ceiling beams that were part of the original hotel have been carefully preserved. Since termites do not like pecky cypress, the beams survived years of neglect when the hotel was closed.

Guests who stroll into the hotel's awesome refurbished Grand Ballroom may imagine the dance floor as it once was—crowded with well-dressed gentlemen and ladies gliding to the musical sounds of famous bands. The room reflects the meticulous efforts that went into returning the once majestic hotel to its original elegance. For two years hundreds of artisans and craftsmen performed the tedious job of repainting, including decorative touches such as the hand-stenciling on the cypress beams in the lobby and restoring wall murals in the dining wing and adding new life to the hand painted ceilings.

When guests settle down in the wicker chairs on the wide front veranda, they cannot help but sense the nostalgia of slower-paced bygone days. On the porch, visitors chat while sipping icy drinks and watching the arrival and departure of hotel guests.

Because the hotel went into decline before its closure in 1974—when rooms went for $7 a night— it took painstaking work to return the sprawling building to its original elegance. For two years

hundreds of artisans and craftsmen spent dedicated hours reviving the original décor.

After the Vinoy closed, the structure became a shuttered derelict loitering on the St. Petersburg yacht basin. All efforts to remove the decaying eyesore from the waterfront seemed doomed to failure; the hotel's demise becoming less of an embarrassment only when it appeared to mirror the decline of the city itself.

The grandest days of the Vinoy were in the years following its opening, in the 1920s and '30s. At that time the hotel, open only four months each year, proved a perfect destination for celebrities and other rich folks who sought to escape harsh northern winters. After a day in the sun, the well-to-do guests shifted to formal attire and enjoyed the pampering

A distinctive crest design that inspired the hotel griffin logo is carved in stone that frames the window outside the Terrace Room of the Vinoy.

The Renaissance Vinoy, adorned in pink elegance, stretches along the shore of Tampa Bay.

developer, years in which the city considered condemning the building with its big broken windows and leaking roof.

It was not until Frederick Guest II came along and spent even more years gathering backing and financing that the creation of a new Vinoy Resort began to seem possible. In 1990, Guest had his financial backing and, as a part of VDC Hotel Partners, entered a joint venture with the Stouffer Hotel Company. Construction for the $93 million renovation project began in the spring of that year.

The new Vinoy Resort offers all the latest amenities seasoned travelers expect to find in a quality hotel. A redesign of guest accommodations in the original building made two rooms our of every three—reducing the total from 375 to 260. A new tower building next to the original hotel offers 102 rooms, giving the hotel a total of 360, plus 29 suites.

Besides its large tennis complex adjacent to the hotel buildings, and a golf course on Snell Isle, the Vinoy also includes a tea garden where guests are free to enjoy the game of croquet. Two spacious heated pools and three outdoor spas complement the hotel grounds. As well, some rooms in the tower building have their own balcony hot tubs.

One of the hotel's four restaurants is named Marchand's Grill in memory of Henri Marchand, the original chef for the 1925 kitchen. Marchand's serves dishes such as pan fried Pompano with citrus and papaya salsa, lamb chops with roasted eggplant and prawns with cumin and lemon butter and risotto. Macadamia nut ice cream dessert is the resort's signature delight.

Handsome leaded glass windows in the Terrace Room face Tampa Bay and the marina. Diners can enjoy breakfast, lunch, and dinner there beneath the hand-painted ceilings and among intricate plaster carvings. Even the decorative base plates have been designed to replicate those used in the early days of the Hotel Vinoy.

In January 2000, during the Renaissance Vinoy Resort's 75th anniversary celebration, the Palm Court Ballroom opened with 11,340 square feet of conference space that can be divided into eight meeting rooms. The addition also includes an expanded parking garage with two "scenic" rooftop tennis courts.

As well as the Palm Court Ballroom and the

of an elegant dinner in the hotel dining room.

During World War II, bad times came for the Vinoy when the Army Air Corps leased it for a training center. Unappreciative solders kicked holes in plaster walls, painted over murals and damaged floors and stair treads. The hotel was badly in need of repair before it could reopen in 1945.

Eventually the Vinoy and its fine ballroom once again became the site of major social events. During the 1950s and '60s, the area's most important receptions, banquets and parties took place at the hotel. But by the early 1970s, lack of air-conditioning and other facilities to serve the more active lifestyle of many vacationers made it apparent that the old hotel would have to change.

But change was slow in coming. After closing in 1974, the Vinoy reopened for only a brief period in 1975. Then came years of struggles to find the right original Vinoy Grand Ballroom, the resort has two others—the 5,000-square-foot Plaza Ballroom adjacent the business center and the 4,000-square-foot Sunset Ballroom that overlooks the hotel's golf course fairways on Snell Isle.

One of the most fascinating bits of architecture uncovered in the Vinoy renovation was a locked wooden door leading to a safe behind the check-in desk. After the discovery, the safe was placed under guard until opened in 1992 at which time 1400 items were found inside, including a silver urn, probably used at tea time in the hotel's early days, and an old-fashioned lemonade holder, discovered wrapped in a 1934 copy of the *St. Petersburg Times*. These items are part of an historic display in the lobby.

One of the best views of the Vinoy Resort is from the St. Petersburg Pier. From there the hotel and yacht basin have the surreal appearance of a panoramic fantasy rising from the past. It is a sight to remember.

Solariums like this one—furnished with a chair and cot—were once available for rent. Guests could enter one of the small buildings, open the roof, and remove their clothing for sunbathing. This seemed quite private until children on the property found they could see inside the buildings from the hotel rooftop using a telescope.

A lavishly decorated entrance greets arriving guests at the Renaissance Vinoy. According to legend, in early years each morning a bellman would light a match beneath the hotel's thermometer to raise its reading. That way guests were more inclined to take their walks and St. Petersburg could claim to be the "Sunshine City."

Vinoy Bell Tower

*T*he Vinoy Park Hotel bell tower was long the tallest structure in the area. Visible for miles, the picturesque lighted tower served as a welcome landmark for fishermen returning home on the waters of Tampa Bay. For years, the illuminated tower also signaled the start of the winter season in St. Petersburg.

Vinoy Bell Tower is a St. Petersburg landmark visible for miles.

Finding Original Hotel Silver

*T*he Renaissance Vinoy Hotel has a small history gallery near the lobby to showcase silver, china, and other memorabilia. Recently, several long lost pieces have been returned for display there.

One is an original 1925 silver pitcher with *The Vinoy* stamped on the bottom. Elaine R. Normile, History Tour Coordinator for the hotel, says the stamp is the identifying feature that indicates the piece is authentic. The woman who brought the two-ounce pitcher to Normile said she had obtained it 72 years earlier in 1927 when she and her husband dined one evening at the Vinoy.

According to the story, before the couple left they asked for water to give their dog waiting in the car. The waiter obliged, bringing them water in the tiny pitcher. "We all imagine the dog died of dehydration," Normile says.

Another woman called to say she had found a Vinoy silver pitcher in an antique store in Rockport, Texas. Because she had once lived in St. Petersburg, the Texan was thrilled with her find.

Asked to return to the shop and purchase the pitcher for the hotel, the woman agreed. Soon after, a four-ounce creamer arrived in the mail along with a "charming" note but no sales receipt. Apparently when the storeowner learned from the woman that the pitcher had been "lifted" from the Vinoy, he got worried. Wanting no problems over the pitcher, he sold it to her for half the asking price, which was what he had paid.

Normile says the woman's note "romanticized about how the pitcher made its way to Texas wrapped in a silk smoking jacket in the '20s or found in a pile of debris in the '70s."

Another woman who had an original china plate from the hotel called to reminiscence about her grandfather who was once a groundskeeper at the Vinoy. While working in the Tea Garden one Sunday morning, he saw a woman, scarf tied about her head and smoking a cigarette, enter the garden. Although she only said, "Good morning" and nothing more, he knew at once that she was Marilyn Monroe. When his granddaughter asked how he knew who the woman was, the man replied, "I knew."

"I'm sure there was no mistaking Marilyn Monroe," Normile says. "It must have been 1961 because there is a famous picture of Marilyn Monroe and Joe DiMaggio taken at The Tides. He was in spring training in St. Petersburg at the time. Marilyn Monroe died the next year."

Normile and other members of the Vinoy staff welcome new additions to the history museum. "People love to romanticize about the Vinoy and (they) treasure their memories of it," she says.

Elaine R. Normile, Vinoy history tour coordinator, shows off some of the original 1925 silver recovered by the hotel for display in its small history museum.

Grove Park Inn, 26 by 20 inches, original pastel by Mary Montague Sikes.

Grove Park Inn
Jewel of the Blue Ridge Mountains

In the late Nineteenth Century when Edwin Wiley Grove began his long summer visits to Asheville, North Carolina, he fell in love with the scenery of the Blue Ridge Mountains that stretched before him like a lovely painted movie backdrop. Grove, a pharmaceutical firm owner originally from Tennessee, became wealthy from his invention of Grove's Tasteless Chill Tonic, a product that contained quinine and stymied growth of the malaria parasite.

At a time when malaria was a deadly menace in the South, Grove's inventions of the tasteless quinine tonic and, later, of a compressed quinine tablet, were lifesavers. Taking advantage of the large railroad terminal in St. Louis to help his company grow, Grove expanded his pharmaceutical business there. Soon afterward, he followed the advice of St. Louis doctors and came to Asheville for vacation. His doctors felt that the mountain climate could possibly lessen his bronchitis problems and also suggested that a doctor from one of the sanitariums near Asheville might actually cure him.

Grove continued to have health problems, but he grew so enamored with Asheville that he bought a residence in the town and moved his family there. Later he purchased a large piece of property on Sunset Mountain and set out looking for the right architect to design the resort of his dreams.

Unable to find anyone to create the hotel the way he envisioned, Grove turned to his son-in-law and business associate, Fred L. Seely, who in May 1912 made a suitable sketch of the proposed inn. Seely relied heavily on photographs of Old Faithful Inn and the Hotel El Tovar on the South Rim of the Grand Canyon in creating his sketch, yet suggested using the native boulders instead of logs in the construction.

In June, Seely and Grove hired J. W. McKibben as architectural engineer and J. Oscar Mills for construction superintendent. As they worked to convert Grove's dream into reality, Seely wrote that the idea of the hotel was to build a home with every modern convenience yet with "old-fashioned qualities of genuineness."

Five individual roofs, each constructed of continuous-pour concrete, would cover the inn. The Inn's highest one, over the Great Hall, was, after its completion, hailed as "one of the largest continuous-pour concrete roofs of its day." Sealed with "five layers of hot asphalt and roofing felt," each roof was covered with six by 12-inch red tile shingles.

Completed in 1913, the massive structure eventually would be called as "the finest resort hotel in the world." A similar image persists today as the Inn continues to attract guests from all over the world.

When modern day guests cross the wide veranda to enter Grove Park Inn, they are opening a door to the past, entering a magical time of early 20th century days when Grove and Seely might be seen strolling through the lobby or admiring the remarkable 7000-pipe orchestral organ built for the Inn by Ernest Skinner of Boston. Although the organ was sold in 1927 for the handsome sum of $75,000, many other

Mountain stone frames the entrance of Grove Park Inn

antique pieces remain sprinkled throughout the hotel to remind guests that the Inn lays claim to the world's largest collection of "authentic Arts & Crafts furniture and lighting fixtures."

Near the entrance, big wooden rocking chairs invite guests to tarry and watch the horse-drawn carriages clop by. Or they may want to observe the meandering comings and goings of other visitors.

The boulders and dark wooden trim of the Inn bring to mind, as revealed by the photographs, the Hotel El Tovar, built on the South Rim of the Grand Canyon. However, Grove was influenced even more by another hotel of the Far West, Old Faithful Inn, in Yellowstone National Park.

Today's visitors to Grove Park Inn find a sport Mecca on the western slope of Sunset Mountain where the resort is built. Tennis buffs enjoy matches on six outdoor or three indoor courts. A sports center includes one squash and two racquetball courts as well as saunas, whirlpools, Nautilus and both indoor and outdoor swimming pools. A beautiful 18-hole course is available as a challenge for golfers of all levels. Designed by Donald Ross, the architect who built Pinehurst #2 back at the turn of the century, the course is backgrounded by spectacular mountain scenery.

The golf course, part of the Country Club of Asheville, was founded in 1893 and purchased in 1976 to make Grove Park Inn a complete resort. Outdoor tennis courts and an historic old clubhouse were part of the club that was originally the Swannanoa Hunt Club.

The misty Appalachian Mountains top off the panoramic view from a dining room window at Grove Park Inn.

A walk around the Inn's sprawling exterior offers a glimpse of the glorious panorama that originally sparked Edwin Wiley Grove's dream. Rolling hillsides and luxurious evergreen trees are visible in every direction. Mt. Mitchell, the highest peak east of the Mississippi River, rises in the distant skyline.

The granite boulders used to construct Grove Park Inn were gleaned from Sunset Mountain and its surroundings. Packard trucks pulled trains with up to 15 wagonloads of huge rocks—some weighing 10,000 pounds—and hauled them to the building site almost 2,500 feet above sea level. Mules, wagons, ropes, and pulleys were all part of the rock moving process before Italian stonemasons and local workers fitted the stones into place. The men were instructed to lay the great boulders so that the time worn faces of the stones would be visible. The boulders were "laid with the lichens and moss on them just as they were found," Seely later wrote.

Built in just under a year's time, the Grove Park Inn began operations in July, 1913, with Secretary of State William Jennings Bryan delivering one of four speeches at the opening, an event attended by "400 of the most distinguished men of the South." Bryan was one of many notables to sign the guest register during the early years. Others included Woodrow Wilson, F. Scott Fitzgerald, Thomas Edison, Henry Ford, John D. Rockefeller, Jr., Herbert Hoover, Franklin D. Roosevelt, and Calvin Coolidge.

Much of the heavy wooden furniture in the 120-foot long hotel lobby was made by Roycroft of East Aurora, New York. The manufacturer hand constructed 700 pieces and more than 600 light fixtures. The huge fireplaces in the Great Hall, as the massive lobby is known, are large enough to hold 12-foot logs. Each fireplace, 36 feet wide, was built with granite boulders weighing 120 tons.

Surprisingly, during its early years the hotel policy discouraged children as guests, prohibited pets, and allowed only quiet talking after 10:30 p.m. According to the hotel pronouncements those days, these restrictions were necessary "to maintain a place where tired, busy people may get away from all annoyances and rest their nerves."

When the United States leased Grove Park Inn during World War II, Axis diplomats were brought to the Inn and detained while awaiting repatriation. In 1942, the Inn was used as a rest and rehabilitation station for the Navy, and then in 1944-45 the Army used it as a redistribution station for soldiers returning from overseas prior to their release or reassignment.

In September, 1955, the Jack Tar Hotels, owned by Charles Sammons, purchased Grove Park Inn and began restoration and renovation. In 1973 the Inn was enrolled in

Mt. Mitchell adds to the view from Grove Park Inn.

the National Register of Historic Places. A major expansion as well as renovation on the Main Inn began in 1978 and these were completed in 1984. The new Sammons Wing and updated Main Inn began year round operations in April 1984. Named for hotel owners Charles and Elaine Sammons, the new wing was nine stories high and built to accent the original building design of Fred Seely. The top floor of the Sammons Wing houses the Heritage Ballroom as well as a lounge, a restaurant, and meeting rooms. These facilities and the guestrooms on the floors below offer an excellent view of the golf course. A completely separate Sports Center opened to the public in December 1985.

An expansion project that began in 1986 added the eleven-story Vanderbilt Wing. The addition gave Grove Park Inn 17,676 square feet of new convention space, more than 50,000 square feet of meeting rooms, and a total of 510 guestrooms. The Grand Ballroom is located on the eighth floor of the wing, and there is also a private Club Floor for pampered guests.

Today the Inn, with its sloping red-tiled roof, continues to fulfill Edwin Grove's dream of a spectacular resort that looked out over the Blue Ridge Mountains. It is well worth a journey to Asheville to see the hotel built of the stone and granite from Sunset Mountain on which it sits.

Grove Park Inn is much like the Ralph Waldo Emerson quote that hangs in the lobby. "Every book is a quotation: every house is a quotation out of all forests and mines and stone quarries and every man is a quotation from all his ancestors."

Grove Park Inn and Country Club is truly a stone jewel of the Blue Ridge Mountains—a tribute to the men of vision who dreamed it, built it, and renewed it for the future.

Furnishing a Mountain Inn

While Grove Park Inn was still under construction, Fred Seely, son-in-law of Edwin Wiley Grove, contracted with Elbert Hubbard, founder of Roycroft Shops in East Aurora, New York, to produce furniture, lighting, and metalwork for the new hotel. Hubbard described the furnishings as "plain, simple, straight-line pieces, genuinely handmade, with quality being the first and last endeavor."

The new dining room would contain more than 400 sturdy oak chairs with the Roycroft shopmark and the Grove Park Inn initials carved into each. Two massive sideboards and four corner servers were among other pieces built for the Inn's dining room. Eight copper and mica Roycroft chandeliers hung from the ceiling.

Copper ceiling lights hung on iron chains from the ceilings of the 156 original guestrooms, and there were two or three Roycroft table lamps in each room as well. The handmade fixtures were crafted so that "not an electric bulb will be seen."

Other room furnishings came from the White Furniture Company of Mebane, North Carolina. The handcrafted solid white oak beds, chairs, tables, dressers, etc. were all built to Roycroft specifications.

Roycroft pieces from the Arts & Crafts period (1895 to 1925) are found in the Inn today. Original lighting fixtures and sideboards can be seen in the Blue Ridge Dining Room.

The Grove Park Inn stands veiled in the forest beauty of the Asheville, North Carolina mountains.

In the past carriage rides provided memorable occasions for guests at the Grove Park Inn.

The Pink Lady ~ Ghost of Grove Park Inn

Like the Hotel del Coronado, the Grove Park Inn is said to have a ghost—a benevolent pink lady. Since early in the Inn's history, stories of unexpected ghostly sightings have surfaced periodically. These appearances are believed to date back to an accident that occurred about 1920 when a young woman, attired in pink, died from a fall in the Palm Court atrium of the hotel.

Joshua Warren, author of the book, *Haunted Asheville*, spent many nights at the hotel in search of the ghost. He also interviewed about 50 people—20 who reported experiencing actual encounters of some form with the Pink Lady.

As with the Hotel Del, one room in particular in the historic Main Inn has been linked to the ghost. That room, two stories above the Palm Court atrium, is room 545.

According to the story, about 1960 a worker who was painting the hotel interior experienced extreme cold chills as he approached the door to these particular quarters. He was so frightened by the incident that he left and never returned to the room.

In 1995, an individual identified only as the Engineering Facilities Manager also had an experience with this particular room. While approaching the room to check a bathtub resurfacing, he felt the hair on his arms and scalp lift up and cold chills race through his body. He says he did not enter the room and that he would never go near it again.

A nightclub manager at Grove Park Inn claimed to have seen the Pink Lady several times. She described the image as dense smoke with a flowing pink pastel color.

The many sightings and other encounters have been experienced by a wide spectrum of guests and employees, ranging from a two-year-old boy to a Chief of Police. The president of the National Federation of Press Women would report more than one encounter with the ghost during her stay in a Main Inn guestroom.

Those who enjoy ghost hunts may want to try out guestroom 545 in the historic Main Inn.

A Side Trip to Rose Hill Plantation

To sample a time when cotton plantations thrived in the Old South, visitors to Grove Park Inn may want to take a side trip to Rose Hill Plantation. This State Historic Site, about an hour and a half from Asheville, is near Union, South Carolina, in the middle of Sumter National Forest.

The plantation, built by William Henry Gist between 1828 and 1832, once encompassed 8,000 acres. During Gist's term as governor, 1858-60, it served as the South Carolina Governor's Mansion. Gist, known as the "Secessionist Governor," was a States Rights activist who four days after his term of office ended signed the Ordinance of Secession that made South Carolina the first state to secede from the Union.

Rose Hill, listed on the National Register of Historic Places, became part of the South Carolina State Park Service in 1960. Park rangers now give tours of the mansion Thursday through Monday of each week.

Spreading branches of ancient magnolia trees flank the front of the mansion where hundreds of rosebushes once bloomed. The roses are gone now, shaded out by the magnolias, but rows of boxwoods serve as a reminder of the once glorious gardens. Originally the plantation was named for its rose gardens, some of which still flourish at the side of the house.

Built of brick made on the plantation, the three-story federal style home has a number of pieces of original furniture. These include a massive four-poster bed and wardrobe in the master bedroom. Two dresses that belonged to Mary Gist, the governor's second wife, also are displayed in that room.

All of the furniture items now in Rose Hill are either original pieces bought back or period pieces from the 1860s. The master bedroom bed and wardrobe never left the house, according to park ranger guides.

Flanked by ancient magnolia trees, Rose Hill Plantation serves as a rewarding side trip from Grove Park Inn. Near Union, South Carolina, the plantation is on the National Register of Historic Places.

An old carriage house, with three carriages that date back to the 1860s, still stands at Rose Hill Plantation.

Although the original flooring for the first two floors was lost to termites, heart of pine floorboards of similar vintage were used to replace them in the 1940s. The original heart of pine flooring remains on the third floor, a setting that was probably used as a schoolroom for the children.

Original hand-carved rope molding adorns the front door entry, and an elaborate spiral staircase faces the entrance.

Oil portraits of William Henry and Mary Gist hang in the entrance hallway. A portrait of his young first wife, Louisa, who died a few days after childbirth at the age of 18, hangs to one side of the dining room. Over the mantle a portrait of Gist's cousin, General States Rights Gist, overlooks the long, completely set dining table. Gen. Gist was killed during the Civil War while leading an attack at Franklin, Tennessee.

According to a park ranger, the art work next to the doorway, inside the master bedroom, was painted by Mary Gist in her effort to cope with family deaths. Two tombstones and a dark-clad figure are depicted here. Of 12 children born to Mary Gist, only four survived to adulthood.

The children's room, just off the master bedroom, enjoys a feeling of light compared to the darkened

This massive four-poster bed is part of the original furniture displayed in the three-story Federal style house.

larger bedroom. An array of doll clothing lies atop a small trunk, and a long christening gown is spread out over a child's bed. A red and green gumdrop tree, left over from Christmas, adds to the room's appeal.

Across the hall, a ballroom occupies the remaining space on the second floor. There are two pianos, one in a small sitting area off to one side.

Behind the mansion, one of the plantation slave cabins remains open to the public. Nearby stands the old carriage house, still sheltering three carriages that date back to the 1860s. All are in need of extensive repairs.

In the 1850s Rose Hill's red brick exterior was modified by a coating of stucco. At some point, the original cedar shake roof was replaced by tin. One of the wooden shakes and a small area of the brick exterior wall are visible on the third floor.

In 1860 William Henry Gist owned 179 slaves who cared for his then 5,000-acre plantation. At the end of the Civil War, President Andrew Johnson pardoned Gist for his part in the secession. The

former governor freed his slaves.

At that time, Rose Hill Plantation was worth only a fraction of what it had been. Unable to farm the property without slaves, Gist rented portions of the land to sharecroppers.

William Henry Gist died in 1874; his wife lived another 15 years until 1889. Both are buried in a family plot near Rose Hill.

Approximately 15,000 people a year visit the Rose Hill Plantation.

To reach the plantation from Asheville, take I-26 to Spartanburg, SC, then take US 176 to Union. Rose Hill Plantation is eight miles south of Union on Sardis Road.

Each authentic piece of furniture at Rose Hill is from the 1860 period.

Part of the Rose Hill gardens visible through a plantation window.

Slave quarters at Rose Hill Plantation, with a large weaving loom.

A striking spiral staircase faces the Rose Hill entrance.

Part III

Hotels of the Mid-West

Gateway Arch, designed by architect Eero Saarinen, is the nation's tallest monument.

St. Louis, Missouri ~ Gateway to the West

A commanding statue of Thomas Jefferson stands as the focal point in the Underground Visitor Center of the Gateway Arch in St. Louis. Easterners may be surprised to discover the tall bronze likeness of the native Virginian.

A turning point in St. Louis's rich history came when President Thomas Jefferson made the Louisiana Purchase in April, 1803. The purchase was the turning point for the nation as well. St. Louis became the Gateway to the West, and a new era of American growth began.

Considered the "greatest achievement" of the Jefferson presidency, the purchase resulted in the acquisition of 828,000 square miles of land extending west of the Mississippi River to the Rocky Mountains, north to the Canadian border and south to the Gulf of Mexico. The size of the United States was almost doubled by the $15 million purchase, suddenly making the fledgling new country one of the world's largest nations.

Two French fur traders—Pierre Laclede and Rene Auguste Chouteau—actually founded St. Louis in 1764, establishing it as a fur-trading center. Begun in what was then Spanish territory, the settlement was named for Louis IX, Crusader King of France.

In 1804, following the Louisiana Purchase, Meriwether Lewis and William Clark launched from St. Louis a 30-man exploration of the Louisiana Territory. Jefferson not only commissioned Lewis and Clark to explore the land between the Mississippi River and the Pacific Ocean, but he asked them also to investigate animal and plant life in the rugged new territory and to encourage friendship with the Indians there.

By 1804, St. Louis had a population of more than 1,000 people, including French, Indian, Spanish, free blacks and slaves, and was regarded as the fur-trading center of America.

In September, 1806, soon after Lewis and Clark returned to St. Louis from their expedition, the settlement became a last stop for outfitting pioneers heading west, determined to establish home and farm sites, mine for gold, or explore the prairies and mountains that lay to the west. Because of its location at the confluence of the Missouri and the Mississippi Rivers, St. Louis became a trade center where many merchants would grow rich selling their goods and furs to those passing through en route to the West.

After Robert Fulton successfully traveled by steam-powered boat from New York City to Albany,

Each year more than two million people visit the Jefferson National Expansion Memorial, a 97-acre national park that contains the Gateway Arch and the Old Courthouse.

a new era of travel and business trade began in 1817 when the first steamboat plied the Mississippi to St. Louis. In the early nineteenth century, river travel—more than one hundred steamboats lining the levee as a common sight—added to the influence of St. Louis. However, in 1849 that same river travel dealt the city a severe blow when a steamboat explosion on the riverfront caused a devastating fire that destroyed more than a dozen city blocks and damaged hundreds of buildings.

By the mid1800s, steam was also powering railroad locomotives, extending passenger service, and eventually adding to St. Louis' importance as a link in cross-country railway travel. Sparked by the 1848 discovery of gold in California, they broke ground on July 4, 1851, for the first railway line west of the Mississippi. Rail service arrived in St. Louis in 1857, bringing with it European immigrants from Germany, Italy, and Ireland.

A delay in rail development came during the Civil War when tracks and bridges were damaged. The first train between Kansas City and St. Louis arrived in September 1865.

The Eads Bridge, completed across the Mississippi River in 1874, established a vital railroad connection between Missouri and Illinois. That same year, a rail connection was established between St. Louis, Dallas, and Houston.

Opposed by steamboat interests, the bridge helped develop the railroads while putting steamboat traffic into decline. Eads Bridge, a National Historic Landmark, still stands and today carries the MetroLink light rail system over the Mississippi.

The new rail connection helped inspire the building of the first St. Louis Union Station that opened in 1875. Almost immediately outgrown, the railroad station was replaced in 1894 with a new Union Station.

Then the most beautiful and largest railroad terminal in the country, Union Station was designed by Theodore Link, winner of a national contest to select a plan. The facility cost $6.5 million to build. The heyday of the railroad terminal came in the mid-1940s when more than 100,000 passengers a day crossed through the station.

By the late 1960s, Union Station had grown more subdued and only 14 trains a day used the once-bustling terminal. The last train left the station on October 31, 1978.

Today, the city of St. Louis delights in its colorful history. Nowhere is that more apparent than at the St. Louis Art Museum.

Created for the St. Louis World's Fair of 1904 (the Louisiana Purchase Exhibition celebrating the 100th anniversary of the Lewis and Clark expedition), the Art Palace housed treasures loaned to the fair by 20 nations. The building stood behind the impressive, yet temporary Festival Hall, a huge structure with a dome larger than that of St. Peter's Cathedral in Rome, and was flanked by two other temporary buildings that were torn down soon after the fair

Carriage awaits visitors to tour historic downtown St. Louis.

closed. Prior to the construction of the buildings, the Fair's exposition company had agreed that at the close it would donate the Art Palace to the city to serve as a public museum.

Opened in 1906, the St. Louis Art Museum inherited a sizeable collection of excellent paintings and pieces of sculpture left over from the fair, including the two statues that now stand by the main entrance. "Painting" and "Sculpture" were first crafted of a non-permanent fiber and plaster substance called staff, but later were redone in marble by the original sculptors, Louis Sainy-Gaudens and Daniel Chester French. One of the country's top museums, St. Louis Art Museum offers free admission, provides excellent children's art programs, and gives daily talks and tours. It is also home to outstanding special exhibitions, including Angels from the Vatican that attracted large crowds during the summer of 1998. Fine dining and a view of the sculpture garden are available in the tastefully decorated museum café.

A statue of King Louis IX of France, for whom the city was named, stands at the top of Art Hill in Forest Park, the site of the Art Museum. Created by artist Charles Niehaus for the World's Fair, the sculpture was recast in bronze at the end of the event and unveiled at its permanent location on October 4, 1906. King Louis IX, who ruled France in the thirteenth century, was sainted a few years after his death and was the patron saint of Louis XV, French ruler when Pierre Laclede founded the city.

Forest Park, dedicated in 1876, was home of the 1904 World's Fair. A glittering array of buildings and other attractions brought in 20 million visitors and allowed 43 countries to offer exhibits. For the Fair, the Smithsonian Institution built a giant outdoor exhibition birdcage. After the fair closed, that spectacular exhibit was left to the city; now the huge cage is part of the St. Louis Zoo, in Forest Park near the Art Museum.

Today the park that extends gracefully across 1,293 acres has a science center, history museum, golf courses, tennis courts, and stocked lakes as well as the art museum and zoo. A popular municipal theatre (MUNY), largest and oldest outdoor musical theater

St. Louis is a sports city. Busch Stadium, home of the St. Louis Cardinals, is often packed with sell-out crowds. It is scheduled to be replaced with a new stadium.

in the country, provides Broadway musical entertainment free for the first 1,500 people who arrive.

Just as when St. Louis was a town of only one thousand people, the heart of the city remains the downtown where visitors enjoy strolling near the Gateway Arch and viewing the mighty Mississippi River. Busch Stadium, home of the Cardinals baseball team, sits almost within the shadow of the Arch. The Cardinals Hall of Fame, beneath the stadium, contains nostalgic old photographs and relics of the team's pennant-winning years, many of them in the first quarter of the century. Mark McGwire's historic 1998 season when he broke a long-standing major league baseball homerun record brought renewed fame to the stadium and to the city.

The magnificent Gateway Arch towers high above the waterfront, impressing visitors from the air, from the river, and from the ground below. On a clear day, the Arch reflects the warm glow of sunlight sweeping like a vein of gold across its stainless steel façade. Reaching a height of 630 feet, the graceful archway stands 75 feet taller than the Washington Monument and is visible for 30 miles.

Conceived by architect Eero Saarinen, winner of a nationwide design contest sponsored by the Jefferson National Expansion Memorial Association, the Arch took four years to build. Unfortunately, Saarinen never saw his dream become a reality. He died in 1961 a year before construction began.

For a small fee, visitors may ride the passenger tram located inside the Arch. Not for the faint of heart, the tram rises to an observation space at the top—a point 60 stories high. From that post a downtown mixture of new and old stretches out like a miniature fantasyland. Built in 1839, the Old Courthouse thrusts its 180-foot high dome against the sky. Steamboats along the Mississippi used the dome for a landmark. Nearby, the Old Cathedral, completed in 1834, contains the tomb of the first Bishop of St. Louis. A short distance away, Busch Stadium spreads its lighted field like welcoming arms.

On the waterway near the Arch, riverboats with colorful names such as Huck Finn and Tom Sawyer are all part of the view. They, like the Arch, are ever-present reminders that St. Louis remains the Gateway to the West.

A statue honoring baseball idol and long-time Cardinal Stan Musial stands outside Busch Stadium.

Spirit of St. Louis

Charles Lindbergh, a famous St. Louis aviation pioneer, made history when he piloted his Ryan monoplane across the Atlantic Ocean in May 1927. Lindbergh's solo flight captured the nation's attention and the world held its breath as it waited for the Lone Eagle to land the tiny "Spirit of St. Louis" in Paris. This record-breaking event made Lindbergh an immediate national hero and gave momentum to the development of aviation in this country.

For many years, those arriving or departing St. Louis by way of Lambert International Airport passed under a replica of the "Spirit of St. Louis" hanging from the airport ceiling. The replica was used for the movie, "Spirit of St. Louis," starring Jimmy Stewart, still popular on many cable television channels. That plane is now on display in the Missouri History Museum, located on the opposite side of Forest Park from the zoo.

Lindbergh's original Ryan monoplane is in the Smithsonian in Washington, D.C.

Union Station ~ Grandest Station in the Nation

When St. Louis Union Station opened in September, 1894, it was considered the "largest and most beautiful terminal in the United States." More than twice the size of the next station, it was built at a cost of $6.5 million.

The architectural design of the station resulted from a national competition in 1891 among architects. The winning entry by St. Louis architect Theodore C. Link was based on a gateway design of Carcassone, a fortified town in the south of France that has stood in some form for 20 centuries.

In about 1240, to strengthen the fortifications of this citadel, St. Louis IX, who ruled France from 1226 to 1270, had his builders construct an outer wall around the inner walled city. Today photographs of the medieval walled city show a relationship between the lines of the towers and design of Carcassone and the architecture of Union Station, which includes a watchtower.

Link, who received $10,000 for his design idea, included three segments in his plans: the Headhouse, the Midway, and the Train Shed. Hotel, ticket offices, waiting room, other offices, and a restaurant were all part of the Headhouse. The Midway provided a covered transfer area for train passengers, and the Train Shed was a roofed area that protected loading platforms.

The magnificent 65-foot barrel-vaulted ceiling made the Grand Hall of the Headhouse an elaborate space to seat passengers. Decorated with stained glass windows, intricate carvings, gold leaf, and Romanesque arches, the hall that once was a waiting area now serves as the Hyatt Regency Hotel lobby, the only Missouri Hotel listed in the 1999 *Historic Hotels of America, National Trust for Historic Preservation*.

St. Louis Union Station saw its heyday during the 1940s when 200 to 220 trains came into the station transporting 100,000 passengers each day.

Serving 17 different railroads, it was known as a "pocket terminal" because all its trains except one entered by backing and required a series of bumpers along the Midway to stop them. A total of 1,900 passenger cars and 12,500 freight cars were changed during a typical 24-hour day at Union Station.

Following World War II, train passenger traffic went into decline as people began to travel more by car and air. Only 14 trains a day used the station by the late 1960s. On October 31, 1978, the last train departed Union Station.

Designated as a National Historic Landmark in 1976, St. Louis Union Station gained a second life with a major renovation in the early 1980s. The Grand Hall with its vaulted ceiling, gold leafing and stained glass was restored to its original grandeur. Retail shops, restaurants and the Hyatt Regency Hotel now fill the spaces once reserved for thousands of passengers passing through each day.

St. Louis Union Station is once again the historical and architectural gem that attracts millions of visitors each year. It stands as a fitting monument to all those brave settlers who passed through on their journeys to populate the American West.

Originally built as the Art Palace for the St. Louis World's Fair of 1904, the St. Louis Art Museum opened in 1906 and features art exhibitions that draw worldwide attention.

Hyat Regency St. Louis, 20 by 26 inches, original pastel by Mary Montague Sikes.

Old St. Louis Lives On at the Hyatt Regency

A bit of old St. Louis lives on in the Hyatt Regency Hotel located within the heart of St. Louis Union Station. Once the largest and most beautiful railroad terminal in the country, Union Station reopened in 1985 following a $174million renovation. The Hyatt Regency St. Louis assumed management of the hotel in 1989.

Sixty-one of the hotel's guestrooms and suites make up the Hyatt Regency Club, set in the original headhouse building that was once known as the Terminal Hotel. Adorned with turn-of-the-century elegance, the Club section features special amenities that include a private lounge where a deluxe continental breakfast and evening hors d'oeuvres are served.

The Gothic Corridor of the old Terminal Hotel has a unique Tudor tracery ceiling. Theodore Link, the architect who, as noted, won the national competition in 1891, created the corridor as a passageway to the main dining hall and to the private dining areas.

A photograph on display in the Hyatt Regency St. Louis shows the Terminal Hotel as it was during early days of the 20th Century.

The hotel entrance as it appears today.

Until the hotel's closure in the 1970s, the main dining room was a Fred Harvey restaurant, known for its culinary excellence and a gathering spot for St. Louis residents. Today the same restaurant, now the Station Grille, is back in operation and accommodates 135 diners. Although the facility no longer features a punched tin ceiling as formerly, the 3200-square-foot space still looks much as it did in early days of the hotel.

A door at the back of Station Grille leads into the small private Theodore Link dining room. There, up to 16 guests can be seated at the long wooden dining table that fills the space. Modern day visitors may want to take a look at the dining room once used by railroad barons of another age, or they may even enjoy dining there.

The hotel lobby is actually the train station's Grand Hall with its impressive six-story, barrel-vaulted ceiling. Carefully restored by Oppenheimer Properties to its original grandeur, the lobby provides hotel guests a view of gilt-adorned Romanesque arches, ornate ceilings, stained glass windows, and a series of modern-day globe lights suggesting an old Victorian railroad terminal.

The magnificent Tiffany stained glass window that overlooks the lobby is regarded as priceless. Three women depicted in the glass represent three major railroad cities of the time—San Francisco, New York and St. Louis (in the center.)

The hotel restaurant menu explains that Theodore Link was a very superstitious man. "Every entry way to Union Station and every window is in the shape of an arch. He believed that no evil spirit will enter an arched doorway. Additionally, he designed everything in multiples of seven for luck: seven ladies, seven windows, seven arches."

The arch over the entrance onto Market Street was originally named the Golden Arch. However, after people discovered that their words spoken in a soft voice on one side of the arch could be heard distinctly on the other side about 40 feet away, the archway became known as the "Whispering Arch."

When the station renovation began in 1978, the four unique statues of women that had once stood in prominent locations around the Grand Hall could not be found. Upon learning that the statues had been sold at auction Oppenheimer Properties put ads in major newspapers nationwide offering to buy back the statues. Amazingly, within a month, all four statues had been shipped back to Union Station, donated by their owners. The statues now stand in their original settings around the lobby.

Today, there are 479 additional guestrooms and suites in the garden hotel building, situated beneath the arched trusses of the original railroad train shed. Twenty rooms near elevators in the new building have been designated especially for single women travelers.

More than 20 additional restaurants and eateries are sprinkled among the many shops at St. Louis Union Station. The 11-acre Festival Marketplace has a picturesque one and a half-acre lake, complete with paddleboats.

Part of a National Historic Landmark, the Hyatt Regency St. Louis is listed in Historic Hotels of America.

Hyatt Regency St. Louis presents an impressive image to the St. Louis cityscape.

The hotel lobby is actually the train station's Grand Hall with its impressive six-story, barrel-vaulted ceiling.

The magnificent Tiffany stained glass window that overlooks the lobby is said to be priceless. Three women depicted in the glass represent three major railroad cities of the time—San Francisco, New York, and St. Louis (in the center.)

The Gothic Corridor of the old Terminal Hotel includes a unique Tudor tracery ceiling.

The Theodore Link dining room sits behind the main dining facility. Named for the architect who designed Union Station, the room is part of the St. Louis "Walk of Fame."

One of the antique train engines on display at old Union Station.

The design for St. Louis Union Station was based on Carcassone, a fortified town in the south of France that has stood in some form for 20 centuries.

Bronze horses grace the lobby of Adam's Mark Hotel. Created by Venetian sculptor Ludovico De Luigi, the stallions, measuring 9 by 12 feet, were cast in Italy.

Adam's Mark St. Louis ~ A Great Place to Meet

From the balcony overlooking the three-story atrium lobby of the Adam's Mark St. Louis, you can see the world coming to you, a recent manager at the facility points out. Built within the shadow of the 630-foot gateway arch, the luxurious hotel combines local history with modern technology to offer an eloquent and enriching experience to its guests.

A pair of magnificent bronze horses greets the guests as they pass through the hotel entrance. Created by Venetian sculptor Ludovico De Luigi, the stallions, measuring nine by twelve feet, were cast in Italy. They stand like proud sentries on a base of imported Italian marble in a flood of daylight that pours through arched windows and reflects on the mirrored columns nearby.

Elaborate Regency chandeliers hang from the ceiling, adding an extra touch of glamour to an already impressive lobby. The 12-foot long crystal fixtures resemble those more likely to be found in an elegant French chateau.

A large portion of the 18-floor hotel was formerly known as the Pierce Building, designed in 1906 by architect F.C. Bonsack and built by an East St. Louis construction company. Known as the "Fourth Street Skyscraper," the 1200-office redbrick and terracotta building was located across from the historic Planters Hotel. The 200-foot-high Pierce Building cost $1.75 million to build—one of the highest private construction contracts of the early twentieth century.

Often considered over the years as a good contender for conversion to hotel space, the building was selected by Fred S. Kummer, president of the Adam's Mark Hotel chain, as the site for renovation and new construction of the chain's flagship hotel. The new facility opened March 31, 1986, with the colorful sending aloft of 910 balloons, symbolizing the number of rooms. That day when officials cut the ceremonial ribbon garland of spring flowers, the Adam's Mark became the biggest hotel in Missouri and the largest such facility between Chicago and Atlanta.

Situated on one city block in downtown St. Louis, the Adam's Mark cost $110 million to build. During the 1993 summer floods, rooms on the top two

Original sculpture dominates Adam's Mark Hotel lobby.

floors—the concierge level—provided an excellent observation point from which to watch the rising waters of the swollen Mississippi.

To preserve a bit of the Pierce Building's history, 10 sets of refurbished bronze elevator doors with their enamel medallions serve as wall decorations. In addition, a handsome bronze mailbox was restored and now handles mail deposits in the hotel lobby. Faust's, one of five hotel restaurants and lounges, is named for an historic 1890s St. Louis restaurant.

Opening onto Chestnut Street, one of St. Louis' oldest streets, the Adam's Mark is a focal point for the historic downtown. The "oldest Roman Catholic church west of the Mississippi" stands nearby. According to a St. Louis guidebook, the Old Cathedral on Walnut Street is considered to be "the first example of Greek Revival architecture in the state." Laclede's Landing, just north of the hotel on the riverfront, is where the city was founded in 1764.

With so much history within easy walking distance, the Adam's Mark is a perfect place for "watching the world go by."

Crystal chandeliers brighten the hotel lobby.

Faust's Restaurant

Through ornate iron gates, Faust's Restaurant opens into the lobby of the Adam's Mark Hotel. Gray paneling fashioned of wood from a 150-year-old barn creates a massive, impressive entranceway. The dining facility retains some of the original timbers from the Tony Faust Restaurant that operated from 1877-1909 in a nearby location.

The early 20th century Tony Faust Restaurant had its own supply of fresh game, ordered railroad carloads of beef from Iowa, and operated a fresh fish market, according to Faust's wine director, Robert Kabel. He claims wine made with new technology in today's restaurant is superior to that of the early restaurant that relied on winemaking practices from the Middle Ages. A page of Kabel's research into the history of winemaking is contained in Faust's extensive wine list.

A library that provides a private dining room for 10 to 12 people is one of the most charming settings of Faust's. A curio cabinet filled with antique china and stoneware graces one wall. Mirrors reflect the images of two large gold-decorated china urns that adorn high pedestals. The dining table's armchairs are upholstered with a handsome fleurs-de-lis design fabric. As a memento, each library dining VIP guest is presented with a framed menu.

Restaurant guests choose from such delicacies as pecan-crusted rockfish, escargot Parisian, Smithfield ham salad, Colorado lamb, and Faust's signature steak. An annual "Lobsterfest" features more than a dozen lobster dishes, including Missouri barbecue lobster made with smoked pepper butter.

Awards for Faust's outstanding cuisine include the 1999 *Wine Spectator*, four AAA diamonds, three *Mobil Travel Guide* stars and a DiRoNA.

Inviting entrance of Faust Restaurant. Set in Adam's Mark Hotel, the restaurant is a St. Louis favorite. Some of the original timbers from the Tony Faust Restaurant (that operated from 1877-1909 in a different location) were used inside the newer version. Gray paneling fashioned of wood from a 150-year-old barn creates a massive, impressive entranceway from the lobby.

Betty Jackson, an Adam's Mark Hotel Ambassador, shows off a private table setting in wine room of Faust Restaurant.

Joseph Diver, Food and Beverage Director, and Robert Kabel, Wine Director, express pride in the Faust Restaurant's menu.

Dining Out in St. Charles

Across the Missouri River, thirty minutes west of downtown St. Louis, the historic community of St. Charles sits along the riverbank. With gas lights and red brick streets, the town is a charming reminder of the time when St. Charles served as the first state capital for Missouri.

Located in the Marten/Becker House, Miss Aimee B's is one of a number of restaurants and gift shops found in the old French Colonial and German architectural-style buildings preserved in St. Charles. On the National Register of Historic Places, the Marten/Becker House was built in 1865 soon after the Civil War ended.

Aimee Becker, for whom the restaurant is named, was born in 1890 in St. Charles. Her Prussian (Marten) and German (Becker) great-grandparents were among the first families to settle along the Missouri River. In 1982 she bequeathed the Marten/Becker house with its original furnishings to the St. Charles County Historical Society. Remembered as a refined lady and gracious hostess, Aimee Becker died in 1984 at the age of 94.

In May 1987, Miss Aimee B's was opened by Judy Howell and Sherry Pfaender and now operates as a Tea Room and Marketplace for local artisans. They purchased the house in 1991.

Dining guests and shoppers who enter from First Capitol Drive come through a main entrance decorated with original iron grille work. The front parlor has a lovely marble mantel set above a coal-burning fireplace. An ornate hand-carved walnut staircase in the front entrance hallway leads to the second floor. The original paintings that adorn the walls of the dining rooms are the work of local artists and are for sale.

A detailed menu features breakfast "delights" including praline French toast with bacon, potato and sausage pie, crab quiche, omelets and other tempting dishes all served with a toasted bagel and cream cheese. "Breakfast desserts" feature such delectable items as peach bombs (whole peaches baked in a piecrust and drizzled with almond butter glaze) and porridge a la mode. The porridge consists of baked oatmeal, eggs, and maple syrup served in a tall glass and layered with ice cream and whipped cream.

The Tea Room features a tempting array of specialty dishes like broccoli lasagna and Florentine crepe pie St. Charles. The crepe pie is described as a wedge of 14 crepes layered with spinach, mushrooms, and Swiss cheese sauce.

Miss Aimee B's is open for breakfast, lunch, and dessert Tuesday through Saturday. Dining there is well worth the trip from downtown St. Louis.

Art in the Courtyard at Adam's Mark Hotel was created by
Brother Mel Meyer, S.M.

The Pfister ~ Milwaukee, Wisconsin

The Pfister, 26 by 20 inches, original pastel by Mary Montague Sikes.

Opening the Doors to the Pfister

When the Pfister Hotel opened its doors more than 100 years ago, Guido Pfister's dream of creating "The Grand Hotel of the West" was at last fulfilled. The year was 1893.

Pfister, an immigrant from Germany, made his fortune as a tanner in the frontier town of Milwaukee. In 1883 a devastating fire destroyed the town's luxurious Newhall House, leaving Milwaukee with a real need for a new grand hotel. With that need in mind, money was raised from stock sales to secure the funds to purchase a hotel building site.

Fate intervened and Guido Pfister did not live to see his people's palace built. After his death in 1889, it was left to his children, Charles and Louise, to resuscitate and fulfill the dream.

When construction began in 1890, the Pfister, designed by architects H. C. Koch and H. J. Esser, was expected to cost about $500,000. By the time the hotel was completed three years later, the price tag had escalated to between one-and-a-half and two million dollars. Completely fireproof and totally electric, the Pfister was the first hotel to boast separate heat controls in each guestroom.

Built in Romanesque Revival style with huge granite columns, the Pfister rose an impressive eight stories. Inside the elaborately ornamented building, 200 guestrooms opened into wide hallways. Sixty-one rooms had private bathrooms, and there were 14 other baths throughout the hotel.

"A grand hotel as a public house was an American idea," Peter Mortensen, Pfister historian, explains. It was "uniting the wonderful ornate architecture of the homes of Europe with democracy. Palaces symbolize hierarchy, but in America the palaces (grand hotels) were open to all of the people," he says. Best of all, you didn't have to be part of the upper class to stay in a palace. The lavish lobby with its oriental-design carpets, ornate columns, chandeliers, and original artwork was a grand salon that served both as a living room and a town square where people often met on business or came merely to be seen.

A walk through the halls of the Pfister reveals corridors much wider than those ordinarily found in modern hotels. When the Pfister was built, the broad hallways enabled ladies and gentlemen, dressed in full skirts and elegant suits, to promenade unencumbered back and forth. The spacious staircases that lead from the lobby up to the next two levels were designed to provide a "fashionable" way for guests to travel between floors.

The goal of the Pfister and other grand hotels of the day was to offer guests such a spectacular experience that it would be all they would talk about once they returned home. Of course they would be anxious to come back the next season, and their enthusiastic descriptions would attract new guests.

Historical photographs and drawings in the Pfister's collection show a drug store located within the hotel that offered guests 24-hour-a-day service.

The Pfister Hotel is a landmark on East Wisconsin Street in Milwaukee

Another feature was an "elaborate soda fountain constructed of beautiful marble and mahogany." One photograph shows a large room filled with rows of billiard tables, along with a notation that the hotel once included "a ladies billiard room and parlor and a gentlemen's lounge, billiard room and smoking lobby." Ladies were forbidden to go into the men's areas, but men could enter the women's.

In the early 20th century, a barbershop was located off the hotel lobby. As cars became a popular mode of transportation, a parking lot for guests was built on the site of the Pfister family home that was once adjacent to the hotel.

Pictures from the 1930s show roof-top dining at The Pfister as well as theatrical performances. Guests could dine and watch a play for $1.50 plus 15 cents tax. In addition, they could dance under the stars, "weather permitting."

In 1899 the Pfister hosted a major political event—a dinner for President William McKinley and his Cabinet. Professional waiters from as far away as Chicago were called into service for the presidential meal. Several years later, after McKinley's assassination in 1901, a memorial dinner was held at the Pfister.

President William Howard Taft was staying in the Pfister when the World War I armistice was declared. Despite streets filled with the sounds of demonstrators, Taft reportedly later told reporters he slept through it all.

Other presidents staying at the Pfister over the years included Harry Truman, Richard Nixon, and Gerald Ford. Actually, nearly every president since McKinley has stayed there.

Today, The Pfister lobby features an elaborate ceiling mural with a blue sky and angelic cherubs. The Latin word "salve" is painted on the walls below each end of the mural. This honorable greeting is inscribed to assure guests from all walks of life that they are held in the highest esteem. When the Pfister was built, salve was understood to mean "a hearty welcome and a fond farewell."

During the hotel's centennial celebration in 1993, Steve Marcus described salve as meaning "people pleasing people." He went on to say, "Without people, you have nothing. The Pfister is all about people—the people who first dreamed of this place, the people who have worked here, stayed here, and visited here."

Originally the lobby ceiling was an all-glass skylight. In 1993 for the hotel's centennial celebration, decorators decided to update the appearance of the lobby by replacing the skylight. However, the look of sky was maintained through the mural with its fluffy white clouds on a sky blue background.

In the 1890s, dining at the Pfister was an all-evening experience. An excellent staff served guests "sophisticated" meals on the best Haviland china,

Guests at the Pfister Hotel enjoy lavish late 19th century décor in the lobby.

especially designed for the hotel by a "prominent artist in the employ of Messrs. Haviland & Company." Guests used elegant Gorham silver in dining rooms filled with the finest original art of the day.

To this day, the Pfister has maintained a reputation for fine dining. Winner of an array of culinary awards for its gourmet menu, the English Room has a tradition of dining excellence. From the lobby, guests descend a wide stairway to the English Room, known as one of Milwaukee's top restaurants.

A menu from the 1930s says the Old English Tavern is "famous for good food at popular prices." During the 1930s and '40s, prominent citizens arrived at the hotel in their chauffeur-driven vehicles to watch afternoon silent movies or to dance in the evening.

The Café Rouge is the spot to enjoy an expansive luncheon buffet on weekdays and a lavish brunch on Sundays. With an elegant setting of sparkling crystal chandeliers and red marble, dining in Café Rouge is a memorable experience.

Diners with a smaller appetite may want to choose the Café at The Pfister. Many of the tables are enclosed in glass along the edge of the sidewalk, lending the atmosphere of a Parisian outdoor café.

Today's guests may enjoy traditional afternoon English Tea in the Lobby Lounge. With its large gray fireplace glowing bright with flames, the scene is reminiscent of years ago when turn-of-the-century Milwaukee residents came for tea and to be seen. Today, the distinctive sound of a capuchino machine echoes across the Lobby Lounge. Strains of classical music played on the grand piano provide a background for quiet tea-time conversation. Occasionally, the television set, hidden inside an ornate cabinet, is opened, and the lobby becomes a sports bar for a few minutes or hours while a local favorite team plays.

How well a hotel does often depends on its management, and over the years Milwaukee's best have found their way to the Pfister.

For years Charles Pfister served as the hotel's general manager. Under his direction, the hotel flourished and became famous throughout the world for its service and accommodations.

Although Charles Pfister never married, he did befriend and mentor a boy by the name of Ray Smith who came to the hotel to work. Young Smith began his career at the Pfister as a bellboy in 1885. He later became the key clerk, managed the hotel cigar store, then was appointed general manager in 1911.

Although Smith left the hotel and worked elsewhere for several years, during major interior renovations in the 1920s he was persuaded to return to manage the Pfister. In 1926, Smith was offered a lease with an option to buy. He also opened the English Room that same year.

The following year, Charles Pfister died, leaving Ray Smith to carry on the family's dream. Smith managed the hotel during the 1930s and until 1944 when his son, Lawrence, bought the hotel from him.

Peter Mortensen, another chef concierge for the Pfister, takes pleasure in a piece of sculpture—one of many in the Pfister's extensive art collection.

During World War II, Ray Smith welcomed hundreds of refugees who fled from war-torn European countries.

During the 1950s, Americans started traveling, and new hotels and motels, built to accommodate automobile travelers, sprang up across the country. Unable to handle crowds of new-style travelers, The Pfister went into decline. In 1962, the bankrupt hotel was sold at auction.

The Pfister was fortunate because Ben Marcus and a group of other respected Milwaukee businessmen purchased it. Marcus and his son, Steve, decided to restore the main building to its "original elegance" and to construct an adjoining 185-room-tower building where the Pfister family home once stood. The tower included convention facilities, a pool, nightclub, and commercial space. Four years and $7 million later, the project was complete.

Another major renovation took place in 1993 to ready the hotel for its centennial celebration. The Pfister now has 307 guest rooms and meeting facilities, including two ballrooms, and can accommodate up to 1,500 people.

Peter J. Iwanowski was appointed general manager of the Pfister in 1996. A native of Germany, he has an extensive background of hotel management in Europe.

A member of Preferred Hotels & Resorts Worlwide, the Pfister has received the "Four Diamond Award" from the American Automobile Association and has been ranked as one of the best hotels in the world by *Conde Nast Traveler*. In 1992, it was accepted in the Historic Hotels of America, a program of the National Trust for Historic Preservation.

Serving Tea and Crumpets

A well-dressed couple sits on a lobby sofa next to the gas log fire, sipping tea and watching people stroll nearby. Behind a long polished counter, a cappuccino machine gurgles. Here and there plates of tortes, scones, and tea sandwiches tantalize both the sight and appetite. Classical music fills the air as a pianist just returned from a concert in Budapest, Hungary plays the baby grand piano.

This is the scene found most afternoons in the Lobby Lounge of the Pfister when a traditional afternoon English Tea is served. Sometimes hotel guests gather not only to dine on special hors d'oerves, but to see and be seen by others. As it was at the turn of the century, the hotel asserts, the Pfister is still the place in Milwaukee to be seen.

Creating a Legacy of Art

More than a century ago, Guido Pfister had the foresight to begin an art collection that today is the world's largest collection of 19th and early 20th century Victorian art permanently on display in a hotel. The 80 or more original paintings and sculptures that decorate the lobby, hallways, ballrooms, and other public areas of the Pfister Hotel are well-worth the interest they attract.

"Dating generally to the years surrounding the hotel's founding, the art collection is an exceptional example of late Victorian taste in America," Russell Bowman, Director of the Milwaukee Art Museum, wrote in his introduction to the book, *The Pfister Art Collection*. "A number of the artists in the collection remain well known today," he adds, citing European artists Eugene Fromentin and Adolph Schreyer and Americans Richard LaBarre Goodwin and Daniel Ridgway Knight as examples.

Knight's beautifully rendered oil painting,

A bust of Guido Pfister, founder of the hotel, graces the lobby.

Many pieces of art and sculpture decorate the lobby and other areas of the hotel.

"Marie," reflects the mood of dreaminess as a pretty young woman sits amidst rose bushes in front of a quiet pastoral scene. Goodwin uses a still life style assemblage of birds with a gun in "Teddy Roosevelt's Door."

"Dick and Harry" are the names of the two impressive bronze lions that have greeted hotel guests since the hotel doors opened in 1893. The lions, a gift from merchant T. A. Chapman, now guard the stairway to the left of the front hotel entrance.

Another gift from Chapman, "Pikemen," by Maurice Denonvilliers, originally stood next to a three-sided fireplace in his store across the street from the Pfister. The two bronze statues now flank the entrance to the Lobby Lounge.

Two important Milwaukee artists from the turn of the 20th century, Richard Lorenz and Louis Mayer, are also part of the permanent Pfister collection. Lorenz was one of the first major artists in the city to have a studio where he displayed his work. Mayer studied with Lorenz as well as in Munich, Germany.

Art in Milwaukee

For many decades art has played an important role in the lives of Milwaukee residents. Today's sophisticated Milwaukee Art Museum, a short walk from the Pfister Hotel, can trace its roots back to the 1880s when Milwaukee was a thriving port city.

At the time most of the city's residents spoke German. Besides their language and culture, they brought craftsmanship to Milwaukee as well as some excellent artists who created panoramic paintings on huge canvases. The work, displayed "in the round," focused on Civil War or Biblical scenes that were eventually sent "on tour" to other communities.

In 1888, the Milwaukee Art Association, formed by the panoramic artists and area businessmen, held its first big public exhibition. That same year, the Layton Art Gallery, designed by London architects W.J. and G.A. Audsley, opened in downtown Milwaukee.

Frederick Layton, the gallery founder, provided a $100,000 endowment as well as 38 paintings for the museum. Many of these can be seen today in the Milwaukee Art Museum's Layton Art Collection.

The art association continued through the years, changing its name and growing in size. In 1918, it became the Milwaukee Art Institute.

Following World War II, a movement developed to build a memorial to those who died in the war. The center would be on the shores of Lake Michigan and would house an art center and the veterans' organizations.

Eventually the Layton Art Gallery and the Milwaukee Art Institute joined to become the private, non-profit Milwaukee Art Center. The Milwaukee Art Museum and War Memorial, designed by Eero Saarinen, who also created the Gateway Arch in St. Louis, opened in 1957 after two years of construction. The museum has the unusual design of a "floating cruciform with cantilevered portions."

In the years after its opening, the art collections continued to grow, creating a need for more gallery space. An addition, designed by Kahler, Fitzhugh and Scott of Milwaukee and built in 1975, houses an impressive collection of American and European art donated by Peg Bradley in the late 1960s.

Part of another major enhancement to the Milwaukee Art Museum opened in May 2001. In the 1990s, with increasing numbers of visitors and interest in expanding youth programs, plans were developed for the new section. In 1994, Santiago Calatrava, a Spanish-born architect, was selected by the museum board of trustees to design it.

His Quadracci Pavilion is the first Calatrava-designed building in the United States. The completed pavilion with a glass-enclosed reception hall and a restaurant overlooking the lake opened in September 2001.

The unique Milwaukee Art Museum and War Memorial lives up to its motto, "to honor the dead, by serving the living."

The Milwaukee Art Museum, overlooking Lake Michigan, is a short walk from the Pfister Hotel.

Describing a Manmade Wonder

The imposing Burke Brise Soleil may one day rival the St. Louis Gateway Arch as a manmade wonder that attracts visitors from all over the world. Designed by Santiago Calatrava, the world-renowned Spanish-born architect, the Brise Soleil is a movable sunscreen that can be raised or lowered to create a shade for the Milwaukee Art Museum's Quadracci Pavilion.

Called a moving sculpture, it gives the illusion of a building with wings. Soon after opening, those wings inspired the "Ideas Take Flight Contest," sponsored by the museum and the *Milwaukee Sentinel*. Contestants were asked to write a 100-word essay describing what the Burke Brise Soleil means to them and to the city of Milwaukee. Prizes included free airplane tickets.

To some viewers who see it for the first time, the Brise Soleil resembles a large ship. That may be because Calatrava finds inspiration in movements from nature such as waves crashing and trees bending. His work seeks to emphasize light and air through the use of glass and steel.

Prior to and during the time of construction of the $100 million addition, the museum had a retrospective of Calatrava's innovative work. Sketches, models, and other documentation of his designs were displayed inside the museum. In his structures he has used slanting pillows of concrete, as in the design of the Lyon Airport Station in France, and glass and steel for the creation of buildings in Toronto, Ontario. The BCE Place Galleria and Heritage Square in Toronto are both built from his designs. He won an international award for his plan for the completion of the Cathedral of St. John the Divine in New York. In 2000 he was commissioned to design the University Centre for Computing and Engineering at Ryerson University in Ontario.

Thanks to Santiago Calatrava, those living in the Milwaukee area as well as visitors can enjoy the spectacular view of Quadracci Pavilion situated on the edge of Lake Michigan. St. Louis has the "gateway to the west." Now Milwaukee has its "wings over the lake."

Part IV

Hotels of the West

Hotel del Coronado ~ *Coronado, California*

Hotel Del, 26 by 20 inches, original pastel by Mary Montague Sikes.

The Hotel "Del" ~ A Trip Back in Time

In 1885, the west was still wild when Elisha Babcock and H. I. Story purchased 4,100 acres of land in Coronado, California. Thus began the building of the legendary Hotel del Coronado.

The two mid-western businessmen first came to the silver strand to hunt the cottontail, quail, and tens of thousands of jack rabbits that lived in the sagebrush. While they rowed across more than a mile of water to the Coronado peninsula, Babcock and Story visualized developing the barren land as a retreat for people who wanted to escape the harsh winters of the eastern United States.

After purchasing the entire Coronado peninsula for $110,000, the men divided the property into lots, cleared away sagebrush, laid a water pipeline from San Diego, created streets, and set up a ferryboat transportation system. A promotional campaign followed to publicize their project. On November 13, 1886, free boat rides across the Bay and a free picnic attracted 6,000 people to a land auction on Coronado; and Story and Babcock recovered their initial investment. In addition, they amassed a huge profit that enabled them to build the Hotel Del, a massive Victorian structure destined to become "the talk of the Western World."

Considered the most luxurious hotel west of the Mississippi River and completed at a cost of $1 million, the Del was built by Chinese workmen who used lumber from 30,000 trees brought by barge from San Francisco. A metal shop, brick kiln, iron works, and lumber plant all were set up on site. Although most of the workmen were unskilled and needed on-job training, the hotel with its 399 rooms was completed in only 11 months.

When The Del opened its doors on February 19, 1888, it was the first structure outside of New York City lighted by electricity. Because of skepticism, there was a back-up gas lighting system that from all reports never had to be used. Thomas Edison even came to supervise installation of the incandescent lamps that were his invention. The electric power plant at The Del was large enough to service the community of Coronado from 1888 until 1922.

With the elegant beauty in the lobby of solid oak pillars and ceiling and an elevator with open gilded cast-iron, the hotel became a Mecca of European culture in the rugged American west. A hand-carved bar was actually shipped around the tip of South America from Europe in 1886 and is still present in the hotel today.

Kept up over the years by renovations including the addition of steam heat in 1897, the original five-story building is still in use. Two newer sections have brought the number of hotel rooms to about 700.

Today, the dimly lit myriad of corridors that wind

With its distinctive red roof and white wooden buildings, the Hotel del Coronado has played an important role in Southern California history since its doors first opened in 1888, satisfying the builders' idea of an "American castle."

and weave throughout the hotel buildings echo with the past. Down those hallways have walked notable public figures such as the Prince of Wales who became King Edward VIII of England and later gave up the throne to marry Wallis Warfield Simpson, a woman he supposedly met at the Hotel Del.

More than a dozen presidents have been guests in the opulent Victorian structure. The first was President Benjamin Harrison who served from 1889 to 1893. His visit in 1891 was part of a presidential train tour to San Diego. The night Woodrow Wilson delivered a political campaign speech in support of the League of Nations, he was an overnight guest at The Del. Dwight D. Eisenhower visited in 1952, and, in 1970, Richard Nixon hosted his first state dinner outside of Washington, DC. In 1982, Ronald Reagan hosted a mini-summit conference at The Del. Scenes from these and other pieces of the hotel's history can be seen in a museum-like gallery filled with memorabilia of the more than 110-year-old establishment. Much of The Del's history relates to books, films, and television. Documentary filmmakers were drawn to The Del as long ago as 1901 when

During the Christmas season, a handsome decorated tree replaces the elaborate chandelier and flower arrangement at the front entrance of the Hotel Del.

they came to record its fascinating beginning. Such stars as George Raft, Ida Lupino, John Barrymore, Lana Turner, Jane Fonda, Shirley MacLaine, Peter O'Toole, Steve Martin, Ellen DeGeneres, and many others have made movies there. The most famous filming at The Del was probably that of *Some Like It Hot*, made in 1958 and starring Marilyn Monroe, Tony Curtis, and Jack Lemmon. Of course, photos from the movie are on display at the hotel.

In 1888, the world-famous New York publisher Joseph Pulitzer was among The Del's first guests. Author Frank Baum was a frequent visitor to Coronado and is said to have been inspired by the Hotel Del to create his Emerald City of Oz in *The Wizard of Oz*. The red shingle roofline and white wood exterior of The Del gives the impression of a wild fantasy from a book of fiction.

Baum designed the unusual lights in the dramatic Crown Room. An architectural wonder on its own, the Crown Room boasts a lovely 33-foot high ceiling

The unusual lights in the Crown Room were designed by Frank Baum, author of The Wizard of Oz. Baum's stories are still read to children in the Crown Room during the Christmas season.

made of sugar pine held together by wooden pegs without nails, posts, or supports. It is one of the largest pillar-free rooms on the North American continent. Baum's exquisite crown chandeliers hang from that ceiling.

Today, visitors to the Hotel del Coronado explore its terraces, balconies, and walkways and are charmed by the salty scent of the Pacific Ocean and the sound of surging waves. The Hotel Del is said to be Southern California's only oceanfront resort. Standing on The Del's white sand beach, guests easily imagine ladies from the late nineteenth century strolling beneath their ruffled parasols. Or they can picture the tent city that once spread out nearby.

The Hotel del Coronado—the realization of two men's dreams—is now listed in the National Register of Historic Places. On a National Historic Landmark plaque dedicated in 1977, these words are engraved: "This site possesses national significance in commemorating the history of the U.S.A."

After John Spreckles, a Coronado founder, brought in boulders in 1906, the beach started to build up.

View of the waterfront from Hotel Del.

The San Diego skyline forms an impressive background as viewed from the Old Ferry Landing in Coronado.

The Del's Longest Staying Guest

*I*n 1892, a woman named Kate Morgan checked into the Hotel del Coronado, and four days later she was found dead on the steps leading to the ocean. She had a gunshot wound to the head. Although the San Diego coroner's office ruled the death a suicide, rumors persist to this day that Kate's estranged husband murdered her.

For more than 100 years since her death, there have been reports of ghostly sightings of Kate Morgan—especially in two hotel rooms, 3312 (Kate's room) and 3502 (her maid's room). These include reports of people seeing a woman clad in black roaming the corridors or standing near a window looking for someone.

Guests and employees have told of hearing footsteps from a room above 3502 that does not exist and also reported hearing gurgling sounds, like someone drowning coming from the bathroom. People have been said to experience cold chills in the room.

Alan May, a San Francisco attorney, was skeptical of the stories until he stayed in room 3312, where, he says, he had enough strange experiences to inspire him to extensively research the hotel ghost. His research resulted in his book, *The Legend of Kate Morgan*. Not only does May tell the life story of Kate Morgan as he uncovers it, but he also relates his own "ghostly" experiences. Strangely enough, May's research uncovers a previously unknown tie linking Kate to May's own family.

In 1992, paranormal researchers from the Office of Scientific Investigation and Research (OSIR) set up equipment in room 3502 and with ABC television cameras rolling allegedly recorded some supernatural activity. According to a newspaper report, Nancy Weisinger, director of public relations at the time, was in the room for four hours that night. She left room 3502 believing "the supernatural really is possible. The ashtray did flip over twice and the glass did shatter in the bathroom," she said. The OSIR concluded it was a case of "classic haunting."

Doubtlessly Kate Morgan is The Del's longest staying guest.

Some memorable views enjoyed by visitors to the Hotel del Coronado. Brightly-colored flowers adorn the edges of many hotel walkways.

Dresses like those worn in the early days of the Hotel Del are on display at the Coronado Historical Museum. "The story of Coronado is the story of a town that grew up around a fairy-tale hotel, and of the well-known and wealthy who came and created a legend," the museum brochure states. The museum is free and open to the public Wednesday through Sunday.

Glorietta Bay, across the street from the Hotel Del, once was the home of John D. Spreckels. Built in 1908, the house was constructed "earthquake proof." (Spreckels had been living in San Francisco during the great earthquake and fire of 1906.) The house was one of the first private homes on Coronado lighted by electricity. It also features brass elevators and a marble staircase.

A Side Trip to The J. Paul Getty Center

*I*n magical serenity, the J. Paul Getty Center adorns a hilltop that overlooks the City of Los Angeles. Opening in 1997, the 110-acre Center features the J. Paul Getty Museum, an expanse of unusual gardens and landscaped terraces, and other buildings that include a research library.

The art museum offers twice the gallery space of the Villa in Malibu that J. Paul Getty opened in 1953 to display for the public some of his European paintings, 18th century French furniture, and Roman and Greek antiquities. The Villa was closed for renovations in 1997.

Arriving at the Getty can be an adventure in itself. The first few months after the facility opened, eager visitors often stood in long lines that stretched far up the hillside outside the complex. After reaching the main gate, people are directed to one of two trams to convey them three-quarters of a mile up an incline to the arrival plaza at the Center. A set of broad steps leads to a glass-walled entrance rotunda by an information desk and two orientation theatres.

The pink-hued travertine stone seen throughout the Getty gives the impression of marble but is really a type of limestone, quarried in Italy. Sixteen thousand tons of the rock, especially cut for the Center, was used for paving blocks and for wall cladding. If a visitor looks closely, he or she may see fossilized remains of leaves, tree branches, fish, and other things embedded when the stone was formed thousands of years ago.

Droves of visitors line up in a misting rain to take a short tram ride to the summit of the Getty Center where views of the city of Los Angeles and magnificent architecture provide a visual feast.

The museum features a cluster of two-story pavilions bridged by walkways. Four of the pavilions house permanent collections, and the fifth offers changing temporary exhibits.

The Getty's famous French furniture and decorative arts are displayed in several beautifully designed galleries. The abundant use of natural light throughout the museum provides daytime gallery lighting similar to that found in artists' studios.

The museum has an excellent full-service restaurant, two cafés, and a bookstore. There is a 450-seat multipurpose auditorium as well. Numerous lectures and artist demonstrations take place each month.

The Center's location in the foothills of the Santa Monica Mountains is off the freeway in Sepulveda Pass. The Getty is about a two-hour drive from San Diego and from the Hotel Del.

Museum admission is free. However, there's a $5 parking fee per car. Parking reservations are necessary for those planning to arrive before 4 p.m. on weekdays.

Architect Richard Meier designed each building in the imposing complex to meet a specific need.

The gardens at the Getty Museum are works of art in themselves.

The J. Paul Getty Museum and its grounds are works of art.

_Two-story pavilions set around an open courtyard provide well-lighted galleries for
the J. Paul Getty Museum's vast art collection. Travertine stone provides
underpinning for walls and buildings._

Hotel El Tovar ~ Grand Canyon, Arizona

The El Tovar, 20 by 26 inches, original pastel by Mary Montague Sikes.

Hotel El Tovar ~ On the Edge of Wonder

Washes of color shift and glow on the craggy facades of the Grand Canyon, transforming the rocks from one vibrant tint to another. At the Hotel El Tovar, on the canyon's South Rim, guests can observe a mist of violet engulfing the morning light and variable colors throughout the day until a rage of glorious orange falls over the canyon at sunset. Year after year, millions of visitors swarm to the South Rim of the Grand Canyon to view the spectacular chasm formed by the erosive power of the Colorado River.

Guests at the El Tovar experience one of the most magnificent canyon views imaginable as they survey the scenic stretch of natural grandeur that ranges from four to 18 miles in width and is about one mile deep. When the sun begins to set, evening diners at the hotel are treated to a wild play of shifting light and shadow on the canyon walls.

Once the Santa Fe railroad reached the South Rim in September, 1901, the line started planning a first class hotel for travelers at the end of Bright Angel Trail. Charles Whittlesey, a Chicago architect who designed hotels all along the line of the Atchison, Topeka, and Santa Fe Railroad, designed the facility, and Fred Harvey Company, the firm that started the first food and rest facilities along the route in 1876, was chosen to run it. According to a Flagstaff newspaper article in 1902, the hotel was to be built on a twenty-acre grant given the railroad by the federal government.

Whittlesey wanted the new hotel to be in "harmony" with the Canyon scenery, so he used native boulders for the foundation as well as for the rockwork and brought huge Douglas fir trees in by rail from the Pacific Northwest to construct the charming 100-room hotel facility. Built on the edge of the South Rim at a cost of $250,000, the El Tovar opened on January 14, 1905.

Following the tradition of naming Santa Fe Railroad hotels for Spanish explorers, developers selected the name El Tovar in honor of Pedro de Tovar, leader of the first expedition by Spanish conquistadors into Hopi Indian country in 1540. Since Hopi Indians guided the expedition group into the "awesome terrain," it seems fitting that in the new hotel, Hopi Indian men later served as bellhops to assist and direct guests.

At the turn of the twentieth century, railroads,

The Hotel El Tovar has been a landmark on the South Rim of the Grand Canyon since 1905.

including the Atchison, Topeka, and Santa Fe, were intent on opening the "exotic" American landscape to tourism. Bringing people in to discover the remarkable sights appeared to have a more promising financial potential than the mining of silver and gold. At the Grand Canyon, trails were excavated and people became guides, outfitters for mountain climbing and camping, and innkeepers.

Built in 1895 about 11 miles east of the South Rim of the Grand Canyon, the Grandview Hotel provided space for early tourists. To meet the needs of even more visitors, the Bright Angel Hotel and a tent camp were constructed soon afterwards on the South Rim.

In 1893 President Benjamin Harrison proclaimed the Grand Canyon Forest Reserve, and in 1906, inspired by a visit to the park three years earlier, President Theodore Roosevelt issued an executive order creating the Grand Canyon Game Reserve. Roosevelt called the canyon the "one great sight … every American should see." Grand Canyon National Park came into being on February 26, 1919, with a congressional act signed into law by

President Woodrow Wilson.

Today, as when first opened, the main entrance of the El Tovar possesses the rustic appearance of a log cabin. The hotel still has charming provincial characteristics in its interior, including log-slab walls and sturdy dark-stained beams and rafters. A big stone fireplace fills one corner of the main lobby, or Rendezvous Room, and wooden floors polished to a shine add to the room's warmth.

When the hotel opened in 1905, it was equipped with electric lights powered by a steam generator. Dedicated to provide first class hotel service as well as show off the timeless panorama of the Grand Canyon, the El Tovar offered its guests fresh fruits and vegetables grown in its own nearby greenhouses. Water was brought 120 miles by railroad tank cars from Del Rio, and milk came from the hotel's dairy cows.

During the 1970s, the El Tovar's heating and cooling system and the electrical facilities were all updated. A remodeling project in 1979 converted a side porch into a dining room overlooking the canyon.

In 1981, a $1.5 million renovation project added

needed insulation and replaced windows, about half of the exterior logs, and decking. An earlier project changed the 100 original rooms, many without baths, to 78 guestrooms, all with private baths.

The Rendezvous Room was redecorated in 1995. Jeanne Crandall, the decorator, studied historical photographs of Navajo rugs and incorporated the colors and design into custom-loomed rug and upholstery material that now adorns the lobby.

Murals on the dining room walls at El Tovar reveal the customs of four Indian tribes. They are the Hopi "praying to Ha-hai-mana," Apache "sun rise dance," Mojave "bird dance or harvest dance," and Navajo "feather dance."

Just prior to the hotel's grand opening, the Hopi House was opened across the street from El Tovar and displayed Fred Harvey's collection of prize-winning Native American blankets. At one time, Hopi Indians gathered each afternoon in front of the El Tovar to perform a ceremonial rain dance.

Whether visitors relax in a lounge chair on a hotel veranda, cross over to the Hopi gift house, or stroll along the Canyon's edge, their visit will be an unforgettable experience. The El Tovar is a hotel that can provide bright, wonderful memories.

The spectacular Grand Canyon with its continuously shifting play of color and light on rock surfaces is the dominant view for guests at El Tovar. Diners can watch the magnificent panorama from windows that overlook the Canyon. The Grand Canyon, north of Flagstaff, Arizona, became a National Monument in 1908 and a National Park in 1919.

The Hopi House, where American Indian souvenirs and artifacts are sold, stands close to the El Tovar.

The Harvey Girls ~ Creating a Tradition

"WANTED—young women, 18 to 20 years of age, of good moral character, attractive and intelligent, as waitresses in Harvey Eating Houses on the Santa Fe Railroad in the West." That is part of the ad run by Fred Harvey in city newspapers in the East.

An industrious restaurateur, Harvey was searching for help in bringing good food service to train passengers along the Santa Fe line. Unhappy with the rough appearance and manners of the male staff at one of his New Mexico establishments, Harvey fired the entire group and replaced them with young town women—beginning the saga of the attractive Harvey Girls who helped civilize the West.

Reportedly, some 100,000 women responded to Harvey's newspaper ads and came west to live in dormitories and earn good wages including tips. Working long hours, they followed strict rules and kept a 10 p.m. curfew.

It was the duty of each Harvey Girl to provide spotless dining rooms, immaculate floors, polished silver, starched and folded linen napkins. A Harvey Girl was not to chew gum and, legend has it that when one did Harvey fired her on the spot.

There were no chipped dishes and no wilted flowers in a Harvey establishment. "Meals by Fred Harvey" were considered so special the statement became a company slogan.

Born in England, Fred Harvey immigrated to America at age fifteen. Starting out as a New York café busboy, Harvey held many different jobs, from working on a packet boat to serving as a mail clerk. Because of his industrious spirit and dedication to high standards, he eventually became general Western freight agent for the Chicago, Burlington, and Quincy railroad. During business trips in the West, he became enraged by the poor quality service and indigestible food served at railroad stops. Unscrupulous restaurant owners who bribed conductors to depart train stations early, making passengers abandon their uneaten food also offended him. The food was then sold to passengers on the next train.

The CB&Q rejected Harvey's ideas for quality lunchroom service, but the Atchison, Topeka, and Santa Fe leased the Topeka station lunch counter to him. Harvey did such a good job that the Santa Fe put him in charge of its hotel and restaurant in Florence, Kansas, and he hired a chef who had once worked for him at Chicago's Palmer House restaurant to run it. As his business grew, he left his job as freight agent to operate his work out of the Hannibal and St. Joseph train depot at Leavenworth, Kansas.

Believing in generous portions of food, Harvey ordered pies cut into quarters instead of serving the traditional one-sixth piece. Traveling often to Europe, he would select and order high quality linen, china, and cutlery for his restaurants.

Since most of his restaurants were located at ATSF stations, food orders were taken on trains prior to their arrivals and telegraphed ahead to the restaurant managers. Smiling Harvey Girls, dressed in neat long black dresses and crisp white pinafore aprons, met the passengers and served them in a pleasant manner, taking care not to let them feel rushed. Unlike railroad station eating situations that had upset Harvey during his own travels, at his restaurants no passenger was left behind when the train departed.

The Harvey Girls signed an agreement not to marry for at least one year. However, it was not unusual for that agreement to be broken. Harvey and these young women are credited with helping to civilize the West by changing the rough reputation of western cattle towns.

By the late 1880s, Harvey House restaurants stood ready to serve passengers every hundred miles along the Santa Fe Railroad. After Harvey died in 1901, his company included 47 restaurants and 15 hotels as well as 30 railroad dining cars. He also operated a restaurant in the St. Louis Union Station that was not on the Santa Fe line. The noted Harvey restaurant at the El Tovar did not open until after his death. Another special hotel, La Fonda in Santa Fe, New Mexico, was held to be a superior assignment for a Harvey Girl.

Sedona Spellbinds Visitors

Like a stunning scene from science fiction, red-orange rock formations jut up against the bright Arizona sky. The spectacular backdrop surrounding the desert community of Sedona, Arizona—a moderate drive from the Grand Canyon—leaves visitors filled with magical memories.

Years ago, when John Wayne and other western movie idols ruled the silver screen, moviemakers discovered and used the natural panoramic spectacle of the Sedona desert in their productions. Mountainous scenery glowed in the distance as cowboy heroes rode on horseback into a glorious sunset.

Today's television commercials capitalize on the exquisite beauty of the Arizona desert. The same celebrated rocks that impressed moviegoers during the middle of the twentieth century delight today's television viewers.

Artists were not far behind the movie studios in discovering Sedona. Painters, fascinated with form and color, could not resist the beguiling attraction of the Red Rock country. In the 1980s artists came to look, liked what they saw and stayed. Not only have several hundred artists moved to Sedona but each year hundreds more visit or teach workshops in the once quiet community.

With the artists came new art galleries in Sedona and the surrounding community. Many are found within Tlaquepaque, an arts and crafts village with the peaceful setting of old Mexico. Others line Highways 179 and 89A.

In recent years, Sedona has become known as a New Age community. Attracted by four energy vortexes located at Airport Mesa, Bell Rock, Boynton Canyon, and Courthouse (Cathedral) Rock, New Age followers come to meditate, recharge their crystal rocks and listen to Indian voices caught up in the wind.

Other visitors come to see if they can witness one of the hundreds of flying saucer sightings reported in the area each year. When eerie lights are reported around midnight above Bell Rock, local residents are not surprised. Such sightings occur regularly, especially those describing a glowing blue light outlining Bell Rock.

Local tour companies have taken advantage of the New Age interests and offer desert tours that focus on energy derived while visiting a vortex. Some companies will devise individual tours that may include a bumpy ride through rustic terrain to a point in the desert where a precarious climb to Devil's

The unique red rock country that surrounds Sedona, Arizona was often the background for western movies.

Bridge begins. To reach the famous landmark, it takes a four-mile trek deep into a wilderness dotted with bark-stripped cypress trees that—because of their tendency to retain water—attract lightning strikes.

A few years ago, construction of John Gardner's Enchantment, a luxury tennis resort in Boynton Canyon, created a stir among New Age people who claim the Indian spirits have been disturbed. Situated within the shadow of the red sulfite rock grouping, the resort has an undeniably spectacular view.

In Sedona, it is almost impossible not to find an incredible view. Every hotel and resort in the area seems to have one. And so do the art galleries that take advantage of their viewpoints by facing wide plate glass windows toward the glowing red rocks.

The restaurant at Bell Rock Inn takes good advantage of the scenic panorama stretching across the horizon, including a captivating view of Bell Rock. For those diners not fortunate enough to face the windows, there is a beautiful stained glass replica of Bell Rock on the opposite side of the restaurant.

A visit to Slide Rock State Park is an essential side-trip for most visitors to Sedona. Clear water careens over dark flat boulders to form a gently slanting fall perfect to attract bathers in summer and photographers anytime. The park features a productive apple orchard and contains original buildings from the Frank Pendley Homestead. After being purchased by the state of Arizona in 1985, the park opened to the public in July 1987.

The unlikely combination of retired people, longhaired artists, and New Age folks in Sedona can be found shopping in the same grocery stores and dining in the same restaurants. Each came to Sedona's Red Rock Country in search of something special—something found in the quiet beauty of the tranquil desert community named Sedona.

Bell Rock is one of the formations that stands out from the landscape around Sedona. It is known as the site of one of four major energy vortexes that draw New Age people and the curious to Sedona.

Bell Rock Inn provides a captivating view of Bell Rock. A stained glass window with Bell Rock as the subject is located in the dining room.

A guide who leads adventurous tourists into the wilderness for remote canyon views straddles rocks at Devil's Bridge.

At Slide Rock State Park, the clear water of Oak Creek careens over dark flat boulders to form a gently slanting fall perfect to attract bathers in summer and camera buffs all the time.

Jerome ~ "Wickedest Town in the West"

Perched on a 30-degree mountainside incline, Jerome, Arizona sits like a precarious bird, wings widespread two thousand feet above the Verde Valley. Gone are the days when copper mining reigned and the town burgeoned with thousands of people. Once known as the "wickedest town in the west," Jerome now boasts a population of less than five hundred good law-abiding citizens.

In the Wild West days before the turn of the 20th century, the community bulged with tents, wooden shacks, saloons, and restaurants. Hastily constructed buildings met the needs of tough men who came to the mountain to dig for copper, but the faulty structures led to three devastating fires that destroyed Jerome between 1897 and 1899.

However, despite fires and ups and downs in copper prices that led to mine closings, for 72 years copper was king in Jerome. Nearly one billion dollars worth of ore was mined there. In 1883 enough gold and silver came from the mines to pay most all of the operating expenses, leaving the copper production as profit. A replica of the extraordinary maze of mining tunnels that still lies beneath Jerome is on view at the Douglas Mansion, now a state historic park museum.

When large amounts of money were needed to finance the purchase of coke for a smelter, Arizona Governor Tritle got James A. MacDonald and Eugene Jerome to back the venture. They formed the United Verde Copper Company in 1882 and, as part of the deal, named the mining camp for Jerome who was the principal financial backer.

By the early 1900s, a new owner named William Clark brought in a narrow gauge railroad, thus helping the United Verde become the largest copper mine in production in the Arizona Territory. Clark also moved the smelter operation from Jerome down to the Verde River Valley into a new, more modern town named Clarkdale.

In 1912 James Douglas purchased the Little

Perched on a mountainside 2,000 feet above Verde Valley, Jerome almost became a ghost town in 1953 when the copper mines closed. The population fell from what was once 15,000 to only 50. Today the population is about 400.

Daisy Mine and its development began. The shell of Little Daisy Hotel and the Douglas Mansion stand today as reminders of the thriving copper production that once flourished in Jerome.

United Verde was taken over in 1935 by Phelps-Dodge. The Little Daisy Mine closed in 1938. Mining ceased at Phelps-Dodge in 1953, turning Jerome into a ghost town and leaving vast quiet spaces where mining equipment once hummed and now sits idle.

In the 1960s an influx of artists revived the dormant community. Today a retinue of hippie artists and others have established a community that in certain ways resembles Soho in New York City. Some of the galleries serve both as home and business for the artists. According to the Jerome Chamber of Commerce, over a third of the town's residents are "artists, musicians, and writers."

One of the best known structures in Jerome is the English Kitchen. Built in 1899, the structure served as a Chinese restaurant until the late 1960s when it became a pizza parlor. Over the years, additions, including a wooden deck, have been attached to the original building. Restaurant guests may order from a varied menu and dine overlooking Verde River Valley with the picturesque San Francisco Mountains gleaming on the far horizon.

In recent years an active historical society has worked to assure that the remains of Jerome's early days on Cleopatra Hill will survive. The old J.C. Penney building on Hull Street is an example. When the first store fell in a 1936 slide caused by underground mining, Penney's moved to an old garage that had escaped destruction. That business closed in 1950, and the building front was restored to replicate the original, complete with show windows.

About a mile north of Jerome a real ghost town has been established for the benefit of tourists who want a peek at life in Arizona a hundred years ago. The trek by foot up the mountain is well worth the effort. As the roadway winds higher, there is an increasingly beautiful view of the landscape panorama that seems to stretch forever.

The walk begins with a close-up inspection of the closed Phelps-Dodge operation. The road passes the remnants of a large swimming pool and several tennis courts that once added a luxurious touch to the premises. A sign atop a 1928 model truck declares that Gold King Mine and Ghost Town are one mile away.

Carefully restored machinery is part of a mining display in Jerome.

Nearing the Gold King Mine that was originally called Haynes, a suburb of Jerome, a visitor may hear a screeching whir of a power saw that periodically cuts through the air. The climb becomes steeper and a little more difficult for anyone affected by the higher altitude. The elevation reaches 5400 feet at the door of a gift shop that houses the entrance to a group of old buildings and relics that make up the ghost town.

Jerome and Gold King Mine are living reminders of wild days of a century past when gold and copper mining and a different style of life ruled the rugged West.

Looking for copper, the Haynes Copper Co. dug a 1200 foot shaft and hit a vein of gold instead. The Gold King Mine, one mile north of Jerome, was originally Haynes, AZ, established in 1890.

The Brown Palace Hotel, 26 by 20 inches, original pastel by Mary Montague Sikes.

Brown Palace Hotel, Denver's Unique Triangle

The triangular-shaped Brown Palace Hotel, built of Colorado red granite and Arizona sandstone, has been a focal point of Denver, Colorado for more than a century. Constructed at Broadway and Tremont in the "Queen City of the Plains," the hotel possesses some of the trappings of a palace.

When the Brown Palace opened in 1892, some of its unexpected decorative touches included the wainscoting and pillars in the lobby fashioned of pale golden onyx. A nine-story atrium topped by a stained glass ceiling, the lobby was not the usual hotel reception area.

Modern day architects and engineers praise the hotel's designers for using the ceiling to bring daylight to the dark interior. During the early years, upon check-in, hotel guests were asked whether they wanted morning or afternoon sunlight in their rooms. The glass ceiling, covering an area of 2,800 square feet, was replaced a few years ago.

When guests gaze up toward the glass, they discover six tiers of exotic cast iron balconies and panels. At ground level, pillars of solid Mexican onyx support a mantel once adorning a giant fireplace that warmed guests when winter winds blew down from the mountains.

Henry Cordes Brown opened the Brown Palace Hotel in 1892, only 34 years after men made rich from gold and silver strikes in the mountains founded the city of Denver. Owner of a triangular lot on 17th and Broadway, Brown hired architect Frank E. Edbrooke to design an "unprecedented" building for the site. The resulting Victorian structure is Italian Renaissance style and is listed on the National Register of Historic Places. The project cost $1.6 million and took four years to build.

The original lamps that hung on the second floor and in the arches when the Brown Palace opened still adorn the hotel. At the time the hotel generated electricity for its operations. That system was replaced during the 1930s.

The same Rocky Mountain Spring water from a 720-foot-deep artesian well that served the hotel in 1892 continues today to provide water for each of the 230 guestrooms and suites. All rooms still look out over the lavishly appointed atrium.

In Victorian times, an underground tunnel burrowed beneath the street, connecting the hotel with the Navarre that served as a well-known bordello and gambling hall. Individual trolley cars rolled under the road, protecting the identities of clients.

An entrance to the tunnel, plus a waxed figure seated in a trolley car, is on view in the basement of the Museum of Western Art located in the Navarre. Paintings and sculpture by Remington, Bierstadt, and Russell are among the 125 artworks displayed in the museum.

The Brown Palace is decorated with much original art and many antiques. The painting, "The Sultan's Dream," by Italian artist V. Tojetti, has hung in the hotel since 1892. Alan True painted the murals

The lobby of the Brown Palace Hotel gives visitors a sense of early frontier elegance.

above the elevators and on the Tremont Street side of the lobby. The work illustrates travel in western America from stagecoach to early airplane.

The mural that originally decorated the ceiling of the Onyx Room, a second floor meeting space, disappeared over the years. In 1980 it was recreated from a word description of "fleecy clouds, chubby cherubs and garlands of dogwood." After submitting his design ideas, M. Lloyd Way received a commission to do a new cherub painting. Using his own children and the children of friends for his models, Way created a new mural with a unique touch.

A carving of Henry C. Brown is found at the right side of the original Broadway entrance. On the building's exterior, carvings of native wild animals adorn the spaces between windows on the hotel's seventh floor. Artist James Whitehouse made the carvings in the 1890s, and the animals have been guardians of Denver ever since.

Those having afternoon tea in the atrium lobby enjoy the strains of harp music that overcome the outside noises of a busy city. Nearby, ever-changing displays of historic relics decorate parts of the lobby.

From old guest registers, photographs, silver and china to historic menus and brochures, the exhibit reveals a bit of Denver's history to visitors.

President and Mrs. Eisenhower were among the Brown Palace Hotel's most frequent presidential guests. The hotel actually served as Eisenhower's pre-campaign headquarters during 1952, and the presidential family often vacationed there during the summer.

The hotel's Gold Room served as an office for President Bill Clinton during one of his official visits. The same room was used by President Eisenhower to write his memoirs.

In 1905 President Theodore Roosevelt who was on his way to hunt bear was the first president to visit the Brown Palace Hotel. Some of the other presidents who followed him include Woodrow Wilson, Warren Harding, and Harry Truman.

Many nostalgic Victorian Christmas cards feature the triangular image of the Brown Palace Hotel. They are reminders of the magical, romantic, and turbulent days of America's West when a new hotel brought unexpected culture and charm to a growing city.

Lobby

Denver and Colorado's High Country

Although some know Denver as the "Mile High City," the skyline rises from a fairly level plain that is a mile above sea level. Set at the foot of the picturesque Rocky Mountains, Denver is a city grown out of America's history—a bit of the real West, wild, rugged, and glimmering with gold prospectors.

When a group of Georgians discovered gold at the foot of the Rocky Mountains, fortune seekers flocked to Colorado. That happened in 1858, not long after the great California gold rush.

A description of the state's mining history and much more can be found in the outstanding Colorado History Museum that features a 112-foot-long timeline describing major events in Denver's history. Several vivid dioramas enhance the exhibits. One depicts the city as it stood in 1860, before fire and later a flood destroyed it. An especially intriguing section of the museum contains portraits and memorabilia from the Tabor family.

Back in 1880 it was Horace Tabor who built Denver's first skyscraper. Known then as the state's silver king, Tabor made a fortune in silver with his Matchless Mine, only to lose it in 1893 when the nation adopted a gold standard. Tabor's illicit relationship with "Baby Doe," the woman who eventually became his second wife, scandalized the country. Augusta, a wonderful five-star restaurant in the Westin Hotel in Tabor Center, is named for his first wife—a lonely woman who retained her wealth in the midst of domestic turmoil.

Built near the History Museum, the Denver Art Museum resembles an ancient medieval fortress. Experts say the Art Museum contains the world's finest Native American art collection, and the first floor galleries house a respectable contemporary art collection.

Not far away, the State Capitol Building gleams beneath a shining dome covered with two hundred ounces of 24K gold. Ironically, it is not the gold but the wainscoting made of Colorado onyx that is truly priceless. The world's only supply of this rose-colored onyx was used in this building and no more has been found.

Other sites of particular interest include the United States Mint, the Denver Zoo, the Botanic Gardens, and the Performing Arts Complex. Free shuttle buses service much of the area, while for a minimal fee, the Cultural Connection Trolley offers unlimited rides. The trolley route extends beyond the downtown area to the zoo and the Gates Planetarium.

Located about thirty minutes from downtown Denver on the Front Range of the Rocky Mountains, the city of Golden serves as a gateway to both the Plains and the Rockies. An authentic western town, Golden was the first capital of the Colorado Territory during the 1860s. In 1873, Adolph Coors came to Golden and with a local partner founded Coors

The Colorado State Capitol building in Denver is modeled after the U.S. Capitol. It features a dome covered with 200 ounces of 24-carat gold. The 15th step on the west side of the building is exactly 5,280 feet (one mile) above sea level.

Brewery, now one of the world's largest. A highlight of a visit to Golden is a tour of the famous brewery. The Colorado School of Mines is another special point of interest at Golden.

Golden's historic buildings, set on or near the tree-lined, brick-paved main street, are also worth a stop. An arch across Washington Avenue welcomes folks to Golden and proclaims the town to be, "where the West lives."

The Table Mountain Inn stands in the midst of the historic downtown. Originally known as Holland House, the hotel first opened in the 1940s. It closed and remained empty from 1988 to 1991 when a $3 million renovation project began. The refurbished Table Mountain Inn opened in July 1992.

Visitors find it impossible to view all of Golden's interesting sites during a short visit. There are many historic houses open for touring, including the Astor House Hotel said to be the "oldest standing hotel west of the Mississippi," and other houses built by

Copper vats gleam inside the Coors Brewery, established in Golden in 1873.

The Denver Art Museum is a 28-side, 10-story-high piece of sculpture. Built to resemble a medieval fortress, it houses 35,000 works of art.

the town's founders from the Boston Company who arrived there in 1859. The Buffalo Bill Memorial Museum and Grave is found west of town atop Lookout Mountain.

The Colorado Railroad Museum created to preserve the history of narrow-gauge Colorado railroads is another favorite stop. Several times a year, a narrow-gauge engine with a few carloads of tourists fires up at the Museum. Along with the National Earthquake Information Center, Golden offers numerous other museums. Red Rocks Park, once regarded as one of the Seven Natural Wonders of the World, is situated to the south of Golden.

Taking Interstate Highway 70 from Golden west toward Vail, travelers cross the Continental Divide through a long mountain tunnel just a few miles past Georgetown. The planned alpine village of Vail provides a change of pace from both Denver and Golden.

In keeping with the village's décor, the Vail Westin features a chateau design and overlooks the scenic waters of Gore Creek. A resort within itself, the Westin features unusual wild game dishes in Alfredo's, one of its restaurants. Some of its unique cuisine items include an appetizer called "carpaccio of charred venison," smoky Colorado pheasant soup and wild game consommé. Sea bass in potato jacket and braised Colorado rabbit are listed among the entrees. The resort is within easy walking or biking distance of Vail Village and Lionshead.

Opened in 1962, Vail has since become known as the largest ski area in North America. Besides the busy ski slopes in winter, the community has several championship golf courses available for public use in summer. The village is full of fascinating specialty boutiques and inviting restaurants. Many businesses close at the end of ski season in mid-April and reopen for summer on Memorial Day weekend.

Traveling east on I-70 and then north on Highway 40, one crosses the Continental Divide through beautiful Berthoud Pass. The new recreational area of Silver Creek is found a few miles beyond the established Winter Park Resort community. Mountainside, a "ski-in, ski-out" timeshare resort, can be seen on a picturesque hillside at Silver Creek.

Another historic community, Hot Sulphur Springs is on U.S. Highway 40, a few miles beyond Granby. The Ute Indians knew about the springs for which the town was named long before the white man came. William N. Byers arrived in 1863 and mapped town streets. Byers originally owned the sulphurous waters that were thought to be particularly helpful in alleviating rheumatism. A Denver physician, Dr. Arnold Stedman, wrote in 1875 that the springs gave the sensation of the body undergoing an immense shampooing and then being kneaded by a giant. The springs are now privately owned and open to the public.

In the early 1900s, Hot Sulphur Springs was a well-known winter resort, attracting skiers from around the world. In 1912 the community hosted the first annual skiing carnival and soon became known as the "birthplace of competitive skiing and jumping" in the state.

The Grand County Museum provides an outstanding pictorial history of skiing in Hot Sulphur Springs. It also offers an outstanding account of the development of the Moffat Railroad line and the

The North Fork Colorado River flows past a scenic hiking trail in Rocky Mountain National Park.

breakthrough in 1927 of the Moffat tunnel. A school built in 1924 and closed in 1964 has housed the museum since 1976.

Established in 1915, Rocky Mountain National Park is north of Silver Creek and Highway 34 with an entrance at Lake Grand. Scenery along the 45-mile-long Trail Ridge Road is breathtaking as it ascends to 12,183 feet. Rangers at the Kawuneeche Visitor Center are especially helpful as are the videos shown in the auditorium.

Tourists who hike along the park trail that parallels the North Fork Colorado River discover unforgettable mountain scenery. In the late spring, snow still blocks portions of the trail and high water makes walking slushy in places.

The beauty of the Colorado Rocky Mountains from Denver, north, west, and south, is spectacular. The breathtaking rugged terrain lures visitors to return again and again, as does the regal beauty of the historic "Queen City of the Plains."

Daredevil rafters ride the rushing waters of Clear Creek at Idaho Springs, Colorado.

Beautiful scenery crowds the roadways at Idaho Springs.

The 11,315-foot elevation at Berthoud Pass brings snow to the mountains even in summer.

Phoenix Mine Reflects Pioneer Spirit

Timbers rise gray and rugged against the dusty Colorado hillside. Above the stark opening in the mountain wall a distinctive weathered sign reads, "Phoenix Gold Mine."

More than one hundred years after gold was found in Cripple Creek, the pioneer spirit lives on in the Phoenix Mine that is both a tourist attraction and a serious mining endeavor.

Alvin Mosch, a gregarious miner with an aristocratic German background, is one of the mine's two owners. As sturdy and rugged as the mine itself, Mosch entertains guests from all over the world with his colorful personal experience stories as well as tales from Colorado history. When he acquired the Phoenix in 1972, Mosch says he was the third man to pay the sum of $5,000 for it.

As he prepares to lead a group of tourists into the mine, Mosch apologizes for having trouble with his left arm. He explains that three weeks earlier a storm came up while he was showing some folks the mine. Not one but four separate lightning strikes reeled four hundred feet inside the tunnel to where he was pointing out gold veins. It was the first time in his life as a miner that lightning struck inside his mine, he says.

Mosch believed the four strikes were "God's message" to him. On one hand he was being told to "shape up and be a better person" and, on the other, he was being shown where a rich pocket of gold ore might be located.

Not long afterward, a very rich streak of gold was found at the spot where two veins come together. The Resurrection Vein now provides more than two ounces of gold per ton and "frequent small pockets of pure gold."

A woman who was in the mine when the lightning struck credits the "Lucky Bucket" she touched earlier in another tunnel with having saved her from harm. An old prospector gave Mosch the large wooden bucket years ago. With the words "Lucky Bucket" painted on its side, it now hangs as an attraction for visitors to touch for good luck.

Mosch says the bucket has been responsible for many new mine discoveries and adds that he often receives letters from visitors who have touched the bucket and found good fortune when they returned home. He tells the story of an older man dying of kidney failure until he came to the mine and touched the favored bucket. Right afterward he got a new kidney, Mosch says, grinning.

Visitors often drop coins in the bucket for extra luck. Each year Mosch donates the money to his favorite charity for handicapped children. He doesn't want to chance losing the bucket's luck by profiting from it.

Mosch 's grandfather, Rudolph Gerhardt von Mosch, was from one of the oldest titled families in Germany, he says. In 1883 at the age of 17 he ran away from home to avoid being sent to the Prussian Military Academy. After crossing the ocean by boat, he walked from New York to Colorado. Totally isolating himself from his German background, Rudolph, who spoke seven languages, insisted that all his children be loyal Americans.

An example of those who settled the rugged western territory, Rudolph von Mosch had a long and colorful career as a Colorado lawman. Since he never drove a car, he would march those arrested, hands in the air and six-shooter against the back, to his pool hall.

Sometimes the walk was as far as 10 miles, Alvin Mosch explains, but the tough sheriff was unrelenting and would not let the lawbreaker drop his hands.

The gold mines, such as ARGO and Phoenix, fascinate visitors to Idaho Springs.

Upon arrival at the pool hall, the sheriff's wife would serve both of them fresh baked bread or pastries. Before releasing the lawbreaker, his grandfather would give him money and warn, "Crime doesn't pay. Don't ever do this again."

Mosch proudly recalls that in all his years as a lawman, his grandfather never once put anyone in jail.

One day in 1952, Mosch's grandfather walked five miles to catch the train to Denver. Along the trip, the 87-year-old man lost his battle with throat cancer and died. Since most of his friends had already passed away the family did not expect many people at the funeral, but to their surprise it took two hours for the crowd to file past his casket. "Perhaps they were all people he had arrested at one time or other," Mosch says, chuckling.

The Colorado pioneer is buried in an old unmarked Indian cemetery near the east portal of the Moffat Tunnel, a project for which he once led the first survey team over the Continental Divide in the James Peak area, his grandson says.

During his lifetime, Mosch's father, Hans, worked in 52 other mines and was one of the builders of the Moffat Tunnel as well. Alvin Mosch tells the story of his father, as a teenager, killing a wild bobcat with a club. The animal's skin then hung on his grandfather's pool hall wall for many years.

The most recent lightning strike is not the only prominent one in the family's history. In the 1950s when Hans Mosch was working with a crew blasting mountainsides at Boulder, he fell ill and did not go to work one day—an unusual event since he was always healthy and never missed work. That same day, he said, lightning struck the mountain and killed the rest of his crew.

Alvin Mosch has had his own share of close calls. Some years ago, he was working on the Senator Silver Mine and had to slide down into a cave. When he skidded through the opening, he explains, he found himself face to face with a mountain lion. Mosch, without a weapon but well-schooled in the ways of the wild, remained motionless, staring steadily at the lion until the animal backed away as far as it could into the timbers at the rear of the cave. Then Mosch stepped out of the cave without ever breaking eye contact with the mountain lion.

Mosch mined silver until the 1983 silver crash. Silver will eventually regain its importance and value as a precious metal, he believes.

When his grandfather died in 1952 on Alvin's birthday, he took it as a sign he must keep on mining.

Today he is still using a Leadville, Colorado jaw-crusher given his grandfather before the turn of the century by Horace Tabor, the well-known Colorado pioneer who developed the Tabor Block in Denver.

Mosch relates that his grandfather met Horace Tabor when he went to Denver looking for a wife and took a job there as a bartender. By then the once prosperous Tabor was a "broken down old man" for whom his grandfather felt sorry. He got to know Tabor well and would give him free drinks. Later on Tabor gave Mosch's grandfather his old mining equipment that he had once used to operate his Gold Run Mine.

A few years ago Alvin Mosch was captain of a sheriff's posse that was pursuing drug-users through the mountains. The posse discovered many of the addicts were Vietnam veterans. Mosch wanted to interest them in a new occupation—that of hard rock mining of molybdenum, the element used in hardening steel. He recalls that Harold Wright, a decorated World War II hero and manager of Henderson Mine at the time, agreed to hire the Vietnam veterans and also to train them in a drug rehabilitation program. The Veterans Administration learned about Alvin and gave him a contract to take the men through his mine in the rehabilitation training.

"That's why I have the red, white, and blue hats." He points to the array of hard hats hanging on the wall by the mine entrance. In order to enter the mineshaft, each visitor must don one of the hard hats. Mosch says the tours with the veterans and their enthusiastic response inspired him to start taking tourists through the Phoenix Mine.

As well as entertaining tourists, Mosch says he learns from them. "I knew about the Berlin Wall coming down six months before it happened," he claims. "I pick up information I can't get in the paper."

If he were to discover a rich pocket of gold in the Phoenix Mine, Mosch says he "could make a million bucks in a couple of months." But he finds the idea of having wealth less exciting than the search to find it. Like his grandfather who refused his German inheritance, Alvin Mosch prefers the experience of the treasure hunt. "Miners who make fortunes often lose them right away," he observes.

Of his mining years he says, "It's never been dull. I never get bored. There's always a new challenge." Without another word, Alvin Mosch disappears into the darkness beneath the sign that reads, "Phoenix Gold Mine."

La Fonda, 26 by 20 inches, original pastel by Mary Montague Sikes.

La Fonda ~ The End of the Trail

*I*n 1610 when Santa Fe, New Mexico was founded at the foot of the Sangre de Cristo Mountains, an inn (fonda) for travelers was already present there. Under order of the viceroy in Mexico City, Spanish Governor Don Pedro de Peralta situated the town on the banks of the Santa Fe River, a tributary of the Rio Grande.

After the Spaniards designed a plaza and distributed lots, they constructed the Palace of the Governors, a town council building, and San Miguel Chapel, believed by some to be the oldest church in the United States. The inn was located nearby on the plaza.

La Fonda is "one of the West's most famous and picturesque hotels." Featuring the atmosphere of a superb 19th century hacienda, the hotel replicates Spanish colonial architecture and has exterior lines similar to the Palace of the Governors found across the square.

In 1630, the Spanish population of Santa Fe was only 250. In 1680, the Pueblo Indian tribes, in retaliation for Spanish attacks on their culture and religion, struck the Spanish missions and attempted to regain control. They destroyed Catholic churches, burned most of the buildings and cut off the water supply, forcing the Spanish residents to seek refuge in the buildings around the Palace of the Governors.

When Mexico won independence from Spain in 1821, a Mexican border policy was reversed and traders were welcomed. Soon a successful trade route between Santa Fe and Missouri was established. The original adobe hotel, constructed at the corner of the new Santa Fe Trail and San Francisco Street, stood ready to welcome the traders, trappers, merchants, and soldiers.

Soon after, in 1828, the discovery of gold in the Ortiz Mountains near Santa Fe brought more people and prosperity for the town. La Fonda's prominence as a place of good lodging and excellent food grew.

In 1846, General Stephen Watts Kearney marched into Santa Fe to claim New Mexico as a United States territory. An extravagant Victory Ball was held at La Fonda and many of those who would shape the history of the West attended.

The buildings in the historic area of old Santa Fe possess an unmistakable look and charm. Some of the most interesting structures, including the Museum of Fine Arts and the Palace of the Governors, overlook the Plaza.

In 1848, Anglo-Americans bought La Fonda and changed the name to U.S. Hotel. During the following years fortunes were made and lost in the hotel's gambling hall. A part of the "Wild West," the hotel back yard was the site of a lynching and, a few years later, the lobby was the site of the shooting of John P. Slough, Chief Justice of the Territorial Supreme Court. In the 1860s, the hotel was sold again and operated as The Exchange Hotel.

During the following years, the hotel changed hands more times, and by 1907 had deteriorated into a boarding house. It was still in operation when New Mexico achieved statehood in 1912. At the same time, Santa Fe became "the nation's oldest capital city." In 1919 the old adobe building was demolished.

A citizen investment group bought stock to finance another La Fonda on the original site in 1923, but that endeavor later failed. Following their acquisition of the hotel in 1925, the Atchison, Topeka & Santa Fe Railroad leased it to the Fred Harvey Company in 1926. La Fonda remained one of the Harvey Houses until 1969 and was one the Harvey

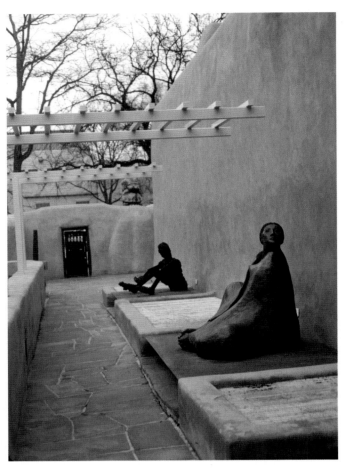

Historic old Santa Fe

The Church of San Jose de Gracia, built in 1760 at Las Trampas. The sign in front of it says it is one of the finest surviving 18th century churches in New Mexico. Las Trampas was settled in 1751 by 12 families from Santa Fe.

Girls considered a "plum" assignment.

When the former parking lot on San Francisco Street was excavated in 1985, the site yielded storage pits from before the Pueblo Indian revolt of 1680. The Museum of New Mexico now has the artifacts for study.

La Fonda's 167 guestrooms and suites feature "traditional Spanish décor." Hand-carved and decorated wooden beds and dressers are among the hotel's furnishings. A 5th floor bar in the Bell Tower advertises "incredible sunset views," and the Plazuela Restaurant offers the pleasant experience of dining in a scenic enclosed courtyard.

President and Mrs. Rutherford B. Hayes, General and Mrs. Ulysses S. Grant, General William T. Sherman, and Kit Carson were among guests who signed the early hotel registers. Hollywood stars including John Travolta, James Stewart, Robert Duvall, Diane Keaton, and Shirley MacLaine have all stayed at La Fonda.

Built in the heart of Santa Fe, the hotel is within short walking distance of many historical museums, art museums and galleries, including the Georgia O'Keeffe Museum.

Georgia O'Keeffe Museum

Georgia O'Keeffe began her love affair with New Mexico in 1929 when she spent her first summer there. In 1949—three years after her husband, Alfred Stieglitz, died—she moved to Abiquiu, making it her permanent residence. She spent the remaining 37 years of her life painting the New Mexico desert and sky and the bones found around her ranch.

The flowers—strange, haunting, beautiful, and unforgettable—for which she is most famous were painted before she moved to New Mexico. Kate Giel, in a Georgia O'Keeffe calendar book of flower paintings, says, "O'Keeffe saw in the shapes and colors of flowers visual equivalents of her life experience." Some of the flowers, mostly painted between 1920 and 1930, are among the canvasses displayed in the galleries of the Georgia O'Keeffe Museum near the Plaza in Santa Fe.

Over a period of more than 50 years, noted landscape photographer Ansel Adams photographed Georgia O'Keeffe many times. "O'Keeffe wears black on most occasions, with enormous distinction," Adams wrote in his autobiography. "The only jewelry I remember her wearing is a simple, silver pin made for her by Alexander Calder. She has the most impressive physical presence of anyone I ever met."

Infatuated with the light and colors of her Southwest home, O'Keeffe painted the desert hills and mountains and myriad skulls and bones of cattle and horses found on the desert floor. In the Georgia O'Keeffe Museum brochure, O'Keeffe is quoted, describing New Mexico as where "All the earth colors of the painter's palette are out there in the many miles of badlands."

With her uncanny ability for close observation, she had a special unmistakable way of abstracting fragments from nature into clear, precise works of art. The structure of the museum that opened in July 1997 is much like some of her art—minimal and very Southwest.

Designed by architect Richard Gluckman, the museum is located just off the Plaza and modeled after the adobe structure of Abiquiu, O'Keeffe's ranch. The interior features hand-trowelled plaster walls, terrazzo cement floors, skylights, and recessed track

When visitors enter the courtyard outside the Georgia O'Keeffe Museum in Santa Fe they experience a momentary feeling of aloneness, possibly inspired by the one small tree that grows there.

lights. When visitors enter the courtyard outside the building, they experience a momentary feeling of aloneness, possibly inspired by the one small tree that grows there. Privately funded and housing the world's largest permanent collection of her art, the Georgia O'Keeffe Museum has close ties with the Museum of New Mexico.

During her long life Georgia O'Keeffe found flowers, seashells, and white bones that intrigued her. She picked them up and took them home to paint.

"I have used these things to say what is to me the wideness and wonder of the world as I live in it," she observes in a brochure quote.

A native of Wisconsin who studied in New York, O'Keeffe will be remembered for her attachment to New Mexico. Her focus and talent brought the ordinary in nature to life in an unforgettable and enduring way—now captured for all time in the Georgia O'Keeffe Museum.

A graceful piece of sculpture stands near the tree in the O'Keeffe Museum courtyard.

Part V

Hotels of Canada

Deerhurst Resort ~ *Muskoka, Ontario*

Deerhurst, 26 by 20 inches, original pastel by Mary Montague Sikes.

Time Travel to Deerhurst Resort

What would it be like to time travel back to the turn of the 20th century? To an era when comfortable vacation lodges graced the banks of rivers and lakes throughout developing North America? To a time when Deerhurst Resort near Huntsville, Ontario was in its infancy?

In those days—more than a hundred years ago—life moved at a more leisurely pace. Without computers, cellular telephones, and televisions to complicate their lives, people paused and enjoyed the rustic scenery of wilderness lands.

At Deerhurst, elegant ladies who could well afford the most extravagant summer vacations strolled along the lawn fronting crystal clear Peninsula Lake. Relaxation was part of the peaceful ambiance of their holiday retreat.

In 1896 Charles Waterhouse arrived in Canada from England and discovered the wonderful rugged Muskoka landscape. Convinced the lake site was a perfect spot to attract summer tourists, Waterhouse built two cottages and a small lodge with 14 guestrooms. In all, the resort contained 18 guest bedrooms as well as a dining room and lounge for smoking.

Because of the lush wildlife setting Waterhouse called the resort Deerhurst, after a grand English estate. In those days the area could be reached only by boat, and to begin its first season the resort had only two guests.

However, Waterhouse's vision did not stop there. He began to invest all his profits into constructing additional cottages and improving the facilities. Even an overflow of guests did not bother him. He erected tents in forest clearings to house the extra people. Because of his determined foresight, the resort's reputation grew to the point that each year before summer began every room was already booked.

Today the rustic beauty of the Muskoka area remains. Golfers share the landscape with birds, squirrels, and other wildlife. Deerhurst Resort spreads luxuriously across 800 rolling and wooded wilderness acres. Its accommodations have grown from the original lodge and dark wood cottages set on four acres of land to include a wide array of villas, suites, and guestrooms.

Major growth in the facilities began in the 1970s and 1980s when Bill Waterhouse and a group of investors took over the resort's operation. A project to "winterize" Deerhurst was completed in 1972 when year-round operations began. That venture included the enlargement of the original lodge to accommodate a conference center, ballroom, and lounge. An 18-hole golf course, outdoor pool, tennis courts, and saunas were added. The guestrooms were improved to include private baths, televisions, and air-conditioning.

An expansion completed in 1990 brought with it a major thrust to attract conventions to Deerhurst. With the addition of the Pavilion sports and conference center, the resort had four indoor tennis courts, racquetball, saunas, an indoor pool, beauty salon and spa, health club, and conference center, all included in the 110,000 square foot complex.

A new championship golf course was also built in 1990. Deerhurst Highlands gives Muskoka a premier course to attract even more golfers into the area. The 7,011 square-yard, par 72 course cost $8 million to build. Making wise use of a setting that includes thick forests, lakes, and creeks, architects Robert E. Cupp and Thomas McBroom and agronomist William R. Fuller designed and

Villas and dining facilities overlook premier golf courses that attract golfers from everywhere.

developed the new course. Lakeside Golf Course, built in 1966 and redesigned by McBroom in 1988, encompasses 4,500 square yards and is par 65.

Following completion of a more than $15 million expansion in 1998-99, the resort now holds 503 bedrooms and conference facilities that offer 30,000 square feet of function space. A renovation and expansion of the Pavilion has brought a new lobby, a four-story hotel wing, renovated indoor tennis and racquetball courts and a new indoor pool. The enlarged conference space and updated amenities have made Deerhurst Resort the premier meeting destination in Ontario, according to resort officials.

Gracious dining is an integral part of the Deerhurst experience. The Pub, placed in the Pavilion, offers good dining value in a casual pub atmosphere. Overlooking the golf course the restaurant has a menu that features a variety of meals ranging from snacks to substantial dinners.

The Lodge Dining Room, set in the original hotel built by Charles Waterhouse, provides a more formal dining experience. Serving international as well as regional dishes, the restaurant is a good choice for theatergoers attending the highly acclaimed musical variety stage show in the lodge ballroom.

Named after steamboats that once delivered guests to Deerhurst, Steamers is the third restaurant on the property. Specializing in Ontario heritage foods, it has a casual log cabin atmosphere.

The winter sports program at Deerhurst includes cross-country ski trails. A shuttle service carries guests to adjacent Hidden Valley where a ski lift and a ski club offer alpine skiing. Snow-mobiling is another winter activity for resort guests. Ice skating on the golf course pond, tobogganing, and even dogsledding are other cold weather features available. For a sentimental trip into the past, guests can also enjoy a ride in a horse-drawn sleigh.

When visitors enter the dark wood-paneled gallery in the lodge, many are intrigued by a nostalgic array of photographs depicting Deerhurst's past. One of them, "Bathing Beauties on Deerhurst Dock—1900," is quick to catch the eye. A picture of Muskoka Road in 1897 shows two people walking along a curving dirt pathway. A photograph taken in 1899 depicts guests seated on the front porch of the original lodge. Other photographs feature guests waiting for steamer cruises, rafting on Peninsula Lake, and playing tennis in 1898 on the site of the present outdoor swimming pool. Seeing all this memorabilia, a guest would find it hard not to become immersed in the past.

With the turn of the 21st century, the early days of Deerhurst seem far away. Women in long, hot dresses. Men in straw hats. Bathing beauties in full suits stretched out on a dock.

Hotels from the turn of the 20th century cause imaginations to soar. It would be fun to time-travel back ….

An easy drive north of Toronto, Ontario, Deerhurst Resort lies in a lush wooded setting in the heart of rugged Muskoka.

Near Deerhurst Resort

Today Deerhurst Resort at Huntsville is a two-and-a-half-hour-drive from Toronto. A trip by rail from Union Station takes three hours. Bus lines, taxis, and limousines all service the popular wilderness area of Canada.

Huntsville had its beginnings as a logging town, founded in the mid-1800s by Captain George Hunt. For many years, the fine resorts of the Muskoka area were accessible only by steamship or railway.

Even in the summer, temperatures are low. Highs in July and August average only in the mid-70s and go down into the 50s at night. In the winter months with highs only in the 20s along with the natural snowfall, conditions are perfect for skiing and sledding.

Algonquin Park, established in 1893, is located nearby. Noted for an abundance of wildlife and towering forests, the park attracts hikers, canoeists, and outdoor enthusiasts of all types. Another close attraction is Muskoka Pioneer Village in Huntsville where early homesteads and pioneer buildings are open to visitors.

The ski lift at Hidden Valley gives Deerhurst's winter guests an opportunity to try alpine skiing.

The Empress, 20 by 26 inches, original pastel by Mary Montague Sikes.

Discover Victoria ~ The Fairmont Empress Hotel

Clothed in ivy-covered splendor, The Fairmont Empress overlooks the inner harbor of Victoria, British Columbia. A beckoning symbol for droves of daily visitors, it forms the hub of a city so English in appearance that tourists may imagine they are in Europe, not Canada.

Much of everything in the provincial capital city has a British flavor, from the extravagant sprawling Parliament Buildings to the luxurious handmade woolen goods so abundant in many shops, including those inside The Fairmont Empress.

For a time the city on the southern tip of Vancouver Island became an imitation England. Its appearance satisfied the fantasies of visiting British officers who, after serving years in the hot isolation of India, were disappointed when they returned to the real "Motherland."

At the turn of the 21st century, the bright, dainty gardens, double-decker buses, quaint cobbled streets, and high tea served in the lobby of The Fairmont Empress continue to maintain the image of the city's romantic past. Afternoon tea at the Empress is a well-known community tradition included as part of many packaged bus tours. Featuring English honey crumpets, sumptuous fresh berries, homemade scones with cream and jam, assorted finger sandwiches, cakes, and, of course, tea, the mini-meal is so popular that reservations are sometimes difficult to obtain.

Victoria has come a long way since its settlement in 1843 as a fur-trading post. In 1858, the town became a supply center for the gold rush, causing the less than 1,000 population to quickly expand. Not long afterward, in 1862, Victoria was incorporated into a city.

In 1898 Victoria's most famous landmark, the Parliament Buildings, officially opened. A tribute to the prosperity of the province, the buildings were designed in "free classical style" by an ambitious 25-year-old architect named Francis Mawson Rattenbury. A giant central dome stands out in the skyline as the dominant characteristic of the Parliament complex that also includes a number of smaller domes. The most ornate décor featuring gold gilt and marble, stained glass windows, and detailed plasterwork is found inside the legislative chamber.

Restored in 1973, the buildings were refurbished with new tiles, plaster, and other interior and exterior embellishments. More than 3,000 light bulbs now provide an impressive nighttime outline of the Parliament Buildings, photographs of which have come to symbolize Victoria.

Named for Queen Victoria, known as the Empress of India, The Empress opened in 1908 and

A totem pole peeks over rows of bright flowers in Victoria, British Columbia.

is among the legacy of buildings designed by Rattenbury. The talented architect echoed some of the smaller domes of the Parliament Buildings in the hotel's structure. From its beginning, the neo-gothic Empress has been a center for glamour and glitz and a focal point for public gatherings and entertainment.

A brainchild of the city's mayor, George Barnard, the hotel was built by Canadian Pacific on reclaimed land atop huge wooden pilings. Using manual labor and horse-drawn carriages, site preparation and construction of the main 116-bedroom building took four years and required expenditures of $1.6 million. With 30-inch thick walls, the new hotel was standing evidence of the substantial building construction accomplished at the turn of the 20th century. An 85-room north wing added in 1910 and another 270-room wing built in 1929 give the imposing structure a sprawling, rambling facade.

In 1966 The Empress was modernized with the addition of efficient heating, refitted kitchens, and updated furniture and fixtures. Hundreds of pieces of hotel furniture were designed for the décor and many more pieces were reupholstered.

Beginning in 1988 the hotel underwent a complete renovation, even closing its doors for six months to expedite the job. Designers researched old photographs and drawings and studied Victorian as well as Edwardian interiors and colors so as to recreate a Victorian era appearance. Workers refinished original inlaid hardwood flooring in the Bengal Lounge and the Tea Lobby. They rebuilt the stained glass dome of the Palm Court, redid all the guestrooms, and carefully restored the Crystal Ballroom, replacing its window glass ceiling with beveled mirrors for a transparent look. They also cleaned the Ballroom's 10 original crystal chandeliers.

At the end of the $45 million dollar renovation, the Empress had a total of 480 guestrooms. Restored antiques and the specially designed carpet, identical to the hotel's huge original rugs, delight everyone including the more discerning guests.

Like the Hotel del Coronado in southern California, The Fairmont Empress has maintained its elegance and its atmosphere despite changes made necessary by modernization. Open fireplaces in the lobby and giant carved beams in the dining room are

Hanging baskets of glorious flowers adorn streetlights in Victoria.

among the elements retained from the hotel's original design. Like the Del, Victoria's landmark has seen its share of visits by royalty and celebrities, including the King and Queen of Siam, Queen Elizabeth II, Winston Churchill, actor John Wayne, and famed writer Rudyard Kipling.

Visitors who travel by ferryboat from Seattle usually need more than one afternoon to enjoy all Victoria and The Empress have to offer. Upon arrival, ferryboat visitors discover an intriguing totem pole standing by the waterfront across from the Parliament. Nearby they may see a Scottish bagpipe player, attired in beret and kilts, wandering along the street intent on his musical performance.

The totem pole is one of many examples of rare Indian art visible throughout the city. The nearby Royal British Columbia Museum houses one of the world's outstanding collections of native Indian art, including a large number of totem poles displayed both inside and out.

Other newer art forms such as soapstone sculpture, carved in a dazzling variety of unusual rock colors, are seen throughout the city both in gift shops and in the many art galleries. The Gallery of the Arctic is devoted to exhibition of native Indian art. Many samples of expensive knitted woolens are sold in stores throughout downtown Victoria. The Cowichan sweater, a product of the Cowichan Indians, is warm, waterproof, and designed using only black and white yarn. Other beautiful hand-embroidered woolen jackets and capes not found in the United States are on sale in Victoria's stores.

Serving a metropolitan area population of about 350,000 people, the city caters to tourism. Because of a moderate climate warmed by the Japanese current, Victoria can boast of flowers in bloom almost year round. In the winter, when other areas of Canada get snow, southern British Columbia has rain.

The city's floral colors, climate, and unexpected beauty all entice tourists to linger a while in Victoria and visit the many parks and gardens, as well as the restored Victorian buildings that thrived during gold rush days. At the end of a day exploring the city, exhausted visitors happily return to The Fairmont Empress for a cup of tea consumed in the leisurely atmosphere of an historic landmark.

Sculpture adorns a walkway leading to the Royal British Columbia Museum.

Victoria Street overflows with people and flowers.

A totem pole outside the Royal British Columbia Museum in Victoria is one of a large collection housed inside and outside the structure.

Building Dining Stations

Back in 1885 William Cornelius Van Horne, the innovative general director of Canadian Pacific Railway Company, undertook the job of enticing the public to explore Canadian wildernesses by way of the recently opened transcontinental railway.

Because wealthy passengers wanted to travel in complete luxury, Van Horne had the Canadian Pacific sleeping cars furnished with wide berths, embossed leather seats, and inlaid wooden paneling. The excellent dining cars offered lavish service with fine linen, silverware, and specialty regional foods.

Unfortunately, because the railway tracks became steeper and steeper in the Canadian Rocky Mountains, the dining cars would shift during the trip, sending expensive dinnerware crashing to the floors. To solve those physical problems, Van Horne decided to build "dining stations" along the tracks. Thus began the Canadian Pacific Hotels & Resorts.

Mount Stephen House, built at Kicking Horse Valley in 1886, was the first of these dining stations. The next year, Fraser Canyon House and Glacier House opened. The first stations were built in Swiss chalet style and marketed as located in the "Alps of the New World."

In 1888, using baronial castles of Scotland for inspiration, Canadian Pacific opened Banff Springs Hotel. The Empress in Victoria, British Columbia opened in 1908. (For many years, Deerhurst Resort in Ontario, built in 1896, was part of the Canadian Pacific Hotels & Resorts.) Architect for the Empress, Francis Mawson Rattenbury also designed many of the chateau "station" hotels.

These luxurious accommodations have flourished over the years and eventually catered to people other than very rich travelers. More hotels were constructed in the 1920s and 1930s, and in 1988 Canadian Pacific Hotels & Resorts bought nine additional hotels from the Canadian National Railway.

That same year Canadian Pacific began a multi-million dollar renovation of its hotels and resorts. The "dining stations," updated with television sets, health clubs, pools, air-conditioning, and other comforts of today's world, continue to thrive.

During 1998 Canadian Pacific purchased Princess Hotels in Bermuda, Barbados, Mexico, and Arizona. Then in fall 1999, Fairmont Hotels was acquired, and the new hotels group became Fairmont Hotels & Resorts. The organization now has "on of the largest collections of distinctive hotels in the world." Van Horne did his job well.

Bright beds of roses are cultivated on the lawn in front of the Parliament buildings that overlook the Inner Harbor at Victoria.

Canadian Gold Rush

*T*he year was 1858. The place—Victoria, British Columbia.
A discovery of large quantities of gold dust in the Fraser and Thompson Rivers had brought in a rush of 25,000 excited prospectors. Many came from California, Oregon, and Washington, and other miners flocked in from as far away as Latin America and Hawaii.

Victoria grew within days from a town of a few hundred to a population in the thousands. A tent city sheltered the new residents who represented a great many nationalities. Many had already tried their luck in California and failed.

Before the end of the year, as much as $1.6 million worth of gold had been taken from the waters. Victoria flourished and grew into a city.

An even bigger gold rush started in 1861 with a strike in the Cariboo region of British Columbia. Billy Barker, the man who made the first gold strike, was suddenly wealthy. A new town named Barkerville shot up. Not long afterward, Barker, like many others of the suddenly rich, lost his wealth and later died in poverty. For a brief period, Barkerville was known as the "gold rush capital of the world." A big fire in 1868 burned most of the town, but by then the boom had ended.

Both the Cariboo and the Fraser River gold rushes were responsible for sizeable population growth on Vancouver Island, where Victoria is established, and in British Columbia. The gold rushes and resultant population increases brought with them a period of lawlessness. In 52 murder trials between 1859 and 1872, 27 resulted in hangings of those found guilty by jurors.

New routes for carrying people and goods grew out of the gold rush. Ranchers started raising cattle to sell, and Catholic priests planted grape vines and fruit orchards. Eventually land, not gold, became the attraction for settlers in the area.

Vancouver Island had become a Crown colony in 1849; the British Columbia mainland became a Crown colony in 1858—the year of the first gold rush. In 1866 Vancouver Island and British Columbia united and, in 1868, the city of Victoria was designated the capital of the new United Colony.

The Prince of Wales, 20 by 26 inches, original pastel by Mary Montague Sikes.

Victorian Charm Found at Prince of Wales

"Easy to find and hard to forget" is a catchy brochure slogan used to attract visitors to Niagara-on-the-Lake in Ontario. The charming, picturesque community is indeed hard to forget and so is the historic Prince of Wales Hotel, situated at one end of Queen Street.

Established in 1864 as Long's Hotel, the Prince of Wales has also been known as the Arcade Hotel and the Niagara House. In 1901 the name was changed to Prince of Wales in honor of a visit to Niagara-on-the-Lake by the Duke and Duchess of York, who later became King George V and Queen Mary.

Treasured old photographs, taken during early 20th century visits to eastern Canada by the British Royal Family, are replicated in the Prince of Wales Hotel brochure. One picture is of the very stately Royal Party that visited Niagara-on-the-Lake on October 16, 1901. Another photograph shows the Prince of Wales posing with his brother, Prince George, during a 1927 visit.

Several times over the years the Prince of Wales Hotel has narrowly escaped demolition, but fortunately it has remained intact at its prime location at the corner of Picton and King Streets. Its unique triangular façade remains a familiar landmark welcoming visitors from Canada, the United States, and beyond.

Late 20th century additions and renovations increased the number of rooms in the original hotel building from 16 to a total of 108. Besides traditional, luxury, deluxe, and premium rooms, the Prince of Wales features elegant suites and superior suites with gas fireplaces.

A short walk from the hotel takes guests to Royal George Theatre on one side of Picton Street and Court House Theatre on the other. The Royal George features a wooden false front and an unexpected interior of Edwardian gilt moldings, golden lions, and red walls. The Court House Theatre provides an intimate setting within a 19th century assembly room. The theatres are home to the annual Shaw Festival where outstanding presentations of the works of George Bernard Shaw and his contemporaries are presented.

The Prince of Wales is another short walk from the Angel Inn, one of Ontario's oldest. Dark hand-hewn beams and sturdy plank floors transport visitors to when British soldiers gathered to dine at the Inn in the early 19th century. Built about 1789 when the town was named Newark, the Angel Inn, then called the Harmonious Coach House, was badly damaged by fire in the War of 1812. After the war, the inn was rebuilt and named Angel Inn for the owner's wife.

Escabeche Restaurant in the Prince of Wales Hotel

An entrance to the Prince of Wales Hotel is visible beyond a mass of foliage and flowers that flourish in the summer in Niagara-on-the-Lake, Ontario.

reflects the opulence of the Victorian age. Featuring French cuisine served with fine china, crystal, and lovely tapestries, the restaurant shows off the more leisurely charm of distant days. Soothed by the background strains of classical music, people were more inclined to break for an unhurried afternoon tea.

For a different menu treat, hotel guests may visit the Churchill Lounge for a spread of unique appetizers such as caramelized onion tart with herb goat's cheese. Here diners will find the likes of steak and kidney pie with mousseline potatoes and cutlet of pork with ratatouille, garlic, and basil crushed potatoes.

Some hotel guests will not want to leave without visiting the Secret Garden Spa. The Spa, with its seven treatment rooms, suggests an English country garden "where delicate wild flowers greet you at every turn."

The Prince of Wales is a "Five Diamond" hotel "that sets the standards" for service and hospitality.

Through the magic of the Internet, people can take a full-featured panoramic tour of the rooms and other features of the Prince of Wales Hotel. One tour takes visitors through a model suite complete with a large balcony, canopy bed, fireplace, and Tiffany-style lamps.

Several suites available in the Prince of Wales offer extra comfort from a fireplace.

The beautiful streets of Niagara-on-the-Lake leave visitors with unforgettable memories.

A Side Trip to Toronto ~ An International City

Visitors to Niagara-on-the-Lake may enjoy side trips to Toronto,
St. Mary's and the area near Lake Huron, and Niagara Falls.

Two hours from Deerhurst Resort and about the same distance from Prince of Wales Hotel is a city to remember—Toronto, Ontario.

Trendy. Cosmopolitan. International. A delightful, sprawling city that traces its history to days of fur traders and Indians.

Modern day Toronto draws people from all over the globe to enjoy the sophisticated lifestyle of the city by the lake. Next to San Francisco, this metropolis claims the largest Chinatown in North America. Some of its people are descendants of the Chinese who helped build railroads in the late 1800s. Although Canada did not permit Chinese to immigrate between 1923 and the end of Wold War II, the policy changed in 1962 to one of equal opportunity. Prior to China taking over Hong Kong in 1997, many wealthy families immigrated to Toronto.

Late spring, summer, and early fall are the times most visitors seek the urban beauty and culture of Canada's largest city. Gone by then are the snow and cold gray dampness that drive scores of city residents to vacation in the Caribbean.

Shopping, of course, is a favorite activity in Toronto, especially in such trendy sections as Yorkville where boutiques, shops, and art galleries flourish. Artwork is displayed attractively, much of it contemporary and giving Yorkville a special appeal for the young, upwardly mobile businessperson. During the 1960s, Yorkville was Toronto's version of New York's Greenwich Village.

Art galleries flourish in other parts of the city as well, including Downtown East, Midtown, Metro North, Beaches, and Harbour Front where a marina and ethnic cafés add to the charm. The Royal Ontario Museum in Toronto is Canada's largest museum. Within its walls can be found an entire Chinese tomb.

Sculptural twin towers form City Hall—a tribute to the city's modern look. A worldwide architectural competition was held to select the designer of the

Toronto's City Hall is composed of twin crescent towers designed by Finnish architect Viljo Revell.

imposing facility. The winner was not a Canadian but Viljo Revell of Finland.

The Canadian National Tower in Toronto is another striking landmark not to be missed. Rising 1,815 feet into the sky, it is said to be the tallest freestanding structure in the world. To gain a spectacular view of the city skyline on one side and of Lake Ontario on the other, visitors ride an elevator to the 1,465-foot observation level. A revolving restaurant offers food, drink, and full view of the city passing slowly by. At night, it's a glittering display. Remarkably, during the daytime the higher elevations showcase a treetop panorama, the signature of Toronto's reluctance to chop down its trees. Not least among impressive features is Toronto's comfortable, efficient and self-supporting subway system, for years the envy of metropolitan areas worldwide.

Besides the multitude of innovative modern buildings, Toronto has its fair share of renovated older structures. The Grange, one of the oldest edifices in the city, built in 1817and modeled after an English Georgian manor house, has been restored to the 1835 period.

For a sense of nostalgia, one need only drive through such vintage residential areas of Toronto as King's Way in Etobicoke. Green lawns and well-kept flower gardens transport you to another era in Canada.

The city's international complexion reveals a wide range of restaurants and ethnic shopping areas. One is St. Clair Avenue West, a section with an Italian flavor. On Gerrard Street East, as many as sixty East Asian Shops cater to Toronto's Indian and Pakistan immigrants.

Vietnamese and Korean neighborhoods show their signs. A Japanese Culture Centre is sited at Eglington Avenue and Don Mills Road. Chinatown lies near the center of the city between Dundas and Spadina, while yet another large segment of the population is Portuguese.

The mixture of peoples blends together into a sprawling metropolitan area thriving with underground shopping arcades, lively restaurants and cafes, theatre, ballet, opera, and a symphony orchestra.

Nathan Phillips Square, with its arches, makes an ideal spot for strolling, taking pictures, or ice skating in cold weather.

The Shakespeare Festival at Stratford is about an hour and a half drive from Toronto. The stone town of St. Mary's with a massive neo-Gothic Opera House is located by the Thames River only a half-hour beyond Stratford.

On the opposite side of Lake Ontario from Toronto, Niagara-on-the-Lake is about a two-hour drive. The spectacular wonder of Niagara Falls is near that scenic community, at one of the Canadian border crossings into the United States.

Whether dining, shopping, or sightseeing, visitors to Toronto can always find something exhilarating to do.

For many years, the steps of the Town Hall in St. Mary's have provided a forum for prominent Canadian politicians.

Bridges across the River Thames provide a pastoral setting at St. Mary's. The town is about two hours by car from Toronto.

Niagara Falls ~ A Spectacle of Wonder

Rushing sheets of water crash and thunder in scenic splendor at Niagara Falls. Picturesque mists rise skyward. Discovered centuries ago by American Indians, the Falls are a wonder of nature rivaled by few other natural sights in North America.

Artists over the years have been inspired by the magnificent spread of powerful falling waters. The work of Frederic Edwin Church is among the most compelling art depicting the Falls. Making many trips, probably on the Erie Canal from his Hudson River home, Church transformed the scene into majestic oil paintings. Among his most famous works are "Niagara," painted in 1857, and "Niagara Falls from the American Side," an eight-and-one-half by seven-and-one-half foot oil painting.

Another well-known American artist, Albert Bierstadt, created at least a dozen paintings of the Falls. Thomas Cole, Frederic Church's teacher, and George Inness also painted memorable works of art using the Falls as their subject.

Many Americans came to know the Falls because of the engravings of artists such as William Henry Bartlett. In 1801 an artist named John Vanderlyn became the first American to paint the falls. He later took his paintings to London and had some popular engravings made from them.

Created twelve thousand years ago, the Falls actually were once seven miles farther down the Niagara River on the Canadian side. Erosion of cliffs beneath the flowing waters shifted Horseshoe Falls and caused the American Falls to increase in size from an earlier, almost non-existent waterfall.

Today the American Falls are 180 feet high and 1,100 feet wide; Horseshoe Falls are 170 feet high and 2,500 feet wide. Together the two form the great natural wonder of Niagara Falls. It is said there are higher waterfalls on the North American continent but none as wide or as majestic as Niagara Falls.

The Falls are manifested on the Niagara River that was formed by the great overflow of water from Lake Erie into Lake Ontario. Starting in 1818, boats provided service between hotels on the American and Canadian sides of the river.

In 1846, a boat named "Maid of the Mist" first carried tourists and goods across the river through the water spray of the Falls. The construction of suspension bridges and then a railroad bridge in 1855 ruined business for "Maid of the Mist." However, the service soon began a new business taking boatloads of visitors on tours of the Falls.

Today people can sit at home in front of a computer and see live pictures of Niagara Falls without even getting wet. The Sheraton Fallsview Hotel, at Niagara Falls, Ontario has three "Fallscams" focused on the Falls for continuous Internet viewing. Two live static views and live auto-refreshing views from a powerful zoom lens are available on the Niagara Falls web site.

In this electronic age, the rushing crash and thunderous sound of falling waters are readily available for all who want to see and hear them. But most people will not want to exchange a cam shot on a computer for the real thing nearby.

Fort Niagara was captured by the British who also burned the city of Buffalo. Three years later, the British returned the land and the modern day border between the United States and Canada was established.

The power and beauty of the churning waters at Niagara have inspired many to challenge the Falls. One

The awesome Niagara Falls cascade in spectacular fashion on the Canadian side near a border crossing that leads to and from Toronto.

Niagara Falls website has a section called "Daredevil Gallery" chronicling thrill-seekers such as Annie Taylor. A schoolteacher from Michigan, Taylor is cited as the first person to go over the Falls in a barrel and live to tell the story. Her feat was accomplished in October 1901, when she claimed to be 43 years old, however, records show her age was actually 63.

In the early 20th century people were permitted to walk out onto an "ice bridge" that forms across the Niagara River during the coldest winters. When the "ice bridge" suddenly collapsed in 1912, resulting in the deaths of three tourists, the practice was discontinued.

Many memorable movies have been made there, including "Niagara," with Marilyn Monroe, and "Superman." Harry Houdini, the famous magician and escape artist, was fascinated with Niagara Falls. Two of his movies, "The Grim Game" and "The Man Beyond" were filmed there.

Indeed Niagara Falls is an awe-inspiring destination that must be experienced in person—it is a vision to remember.

Niagara Falls

Part VI

Hotels of the Caribbean

Rose Hall Great House, 20 by 26 inches, original pastel by Mary Montague Sikes.

MARY MONTAGUE SIKES

Wyndham Rose Hall Resort

The Wyndham Rose Hall Resort sits like an elegant lady on the edge of the Caribbean Sea where clear blue green waters and sugar white sands invite guests to take off their shoes and enjoy the carefree ambience of Jamaica. Set on 400 acres of the famous Rose Hall sugar plantation, the 488-room resort is located near Montego Bay, between the sea and the Blue Mountains.

In addition to its three interconnected swimming pools, the Wyndham Rose Hall has a second pool area, "Sugar Mill Falls," said to be the "most distinctive water complex in Jamaica and one of the biggest man-made attractions in the Caribbean." The 110,000 square-foot complex features three terraced pools, a 280-foot waterslide, and three Jacuzzi hot tubs. Canals with waterfalls meander through the water park that offers architectural features based on the original Rose Hall estate.

The resort maintains its own unique par 72 golf course and six tennis courts, lighted for evening play. Free snorkeling, ocean kayaks, and a glass bottom boat all provide additional activities for the entire family.

Guests may enjoy breakfast and a dinner buffet in the Terrace Restaurant. Java Blue Mountain Café offers a continental menu for breakfast, lunch, and dinner. For a Mediterranean cuisine, guests may choose dinner six nights a week at Ambrosia at the golf course Club House. The Pool Grille and Mangoes at Sugar Mill Falls provide casual dining for sun lovers.

A trip to Jamaica would not be complete without a side trip to Ocho Rios to visit Dunn's River Falls. The picturesque falls are about an hour's drive from the Wyndham.

Cascading six hundred feet over time-smoothed rocks, the waterfalls meet the sea, passing through a gentle rain forest along the way. The climb up the falls is a challenge few visitors can resist, but for those who wish to stay dry there are cement steps and a series of observation decks that wind along the side of the rocks that edge the scenic wonder.

The Wyndham Rose Hall lies nestled in a grove of lovely palm trees overlooking the Caribbean Sea.

Nearby the falls, Prospect Plantation is a working agricultural enterprise that offers daily tours. An open jitney bus, powered by a farm tractor, takes tourists along trails that cross through fields of sugarcane, pineapples, bananas, and coffee, and then past exotic pimento, almond, orange, and lime trees.

Breathtaking views of the White River Gorge appear through the trees. The charming Prospect Chapel, where students from a nearby college worship, is a surprise part of the plantation landscape. Built from weathered wood and yellow stone, it stands out against the lush green foliage.

At Chukka Cove Farm the novice equestrian may select a gentle horse for a sightseeing tour guided by a veteran jockey. Riders have the choice of exploring mountainous regions or trotting by polo fields on seaside trails where the sound and sight of crashing waves proves exhilarating. The path bends past Devil's Island where years ago actors Dustin Hoffman and the late Steve McQueen filmed the popular movie, "Papillion."

The Greenwood Great House that once belonged to a cousin of the famous poet, Elizabeth Barrett Browning, is near the Wyndham. However, because of its proximity to Rose Hall Great House, the site of murder and mysterious happenings during the days of slavery, Wyndham Rose Hall Resort may be the most compelling destination in all of Jamaica.

A view from a Wyndham window includes a pool, the beach, and the Caribbean.

Rose Hall ~ Home of the White Witch

Like a lonely sentinel, Rose Hall Great House sits perched on a grassy hillside overlooking the Caribbean Sea. Built in the days when sugarcane and rich plantations thrived in Jamaica, the old mansion now looms as a ghostly reminder of the haunting story of the "white witch."

Travelers along the road to Montego Bay who see the forlorn house with its dark windows and dramatic arches may imagine the notorious Annie Palmer peering out from her bedroom, still keeping vigil over the sprawling plantation grounds. They may even believe they see her petite form, clad in a long flowing gown, climbing the wide stone steps. Legend blames Annie for the murders of her three husbands and for a multitude of other cruel and brutal acts against her unfortunate plantation slaves.

Plans for Rose Hall Great House date back more than two and a half centuries to 1746 when Henry Fanning discovered the scenic sugarcane fields that bordered a long stretch of Caribbean coastline. That year Fanning married Rosa Kelly, for whom the mansion was eventually named, but he died six months later without realizing his dream of building a stately house on his plantation fields. It was not until 1750 that George Ash, Rosa's second husband, began construction of the white stone mansion. Ash died two years later and that same year the star-crossed Rosa married her third husband, Norwood Witter. Rosa then suffered through an unhappy 13-year marriage that ended with Norwood's death in 1766.

Between 1770 and 1780, John Palmer, Rosa's fourth husband, completed the Great House project. Palmer, the representative of King George III to Jamaica, owned the neighboring Palmyra estate. Outliving both Rosa and another wife as well, John Palmer died in 1797, leaving Rose Hall and Palmyra to his sons, John and James. When both men died in England without children and without ever having visited Jamaica or Rose Hall, the property reverted to John Palmer's great nephew, John Rose Palmer. Young Palmer took an immediate interest in his inheritance and sailed from England to take care of the long-neglected properties.

Rose Hall Great House, built in 1770-80 and restored in 1971, overlooks the major coastal highway that runs from Montego Bay to Ocho Rios. It is a short walk from the Wyndham Rose Hall Resort.

Annie Palmer's bedroom has a dramatic rose motif.

In 1820 Palmer met 18-year-old Annie May Paterson and married her. The beautiful English-born Annie is believed to have grown up in Haiti under the care of a voodoo high priestess who taught her many unusual black magic practices and permitted her to attend forbidden voodoo orgies.

According to legend, John Rose Palmer may have been a drunk who beat Annie and caused her to have a miscarriage. Some say mistreatment at his hands may have led to Annie's cruelty.

In any case, only three years after their marriage Annie poisoned Palmer and then, according to legend, had flogged to death the slave who helped her murder him. Annie strangled her second husband and stabbed to death her third.

Fearing the power of the "white witch," the village obeahman tried unsuccessfully to have her killed. Annie continued her torturous ways and was often seen at night dressed in a man's clothing and riding a black horse.

Neighboring plantation owners, including the Barretts (ancestors of poet Elizabeth Barrett Browning) shunned Annie Palmer. With good reason her own slaves despised her and believed that an evil spirit haunted Rose Hall.

According to tales that spread through Jamaica, Annie took many of her slaves for lovers, then murdered them when she developed a new interest. Folks claim that until Rose Hall fell into ruin, a large bloodstain from one of the murdered men could clearly be seen on the floor. After an uprising when the sugarcane fields were burned, Annie herself was murdered in her own bedroom by her slaves.

Annie Palmer is buried in the center of the garden by the east wing of Rose Hall. A visit to the gravesite and the singing of a ballad, "Curse of Rose Hall," by a tour guide, have been popular parts of the Great House Tour.

After Annie's death, because of the dark history of the Great House no one would live there. Rose Hall fell into decay and its furnishings vanished. One owner stripped away most of the building's interior and used the materials to construct a new house in Kingston. Over the years the roof deteriorated and parts of the exterior walls crumbled. The porticos, verandas, and even the staircase disappeared.

From the 1930s until the 1960s Rose Hall stood as a derelict reminder of long-ago opulence. Then John Rollins, former lieutenant governor of Delaware, discovered the Rose Hall Great House and purchased the decaying estate.

Determined to restore the house to its original state of elegance, Rollins employed an architect, the late Tom Concannon, to study and refurbish Rose

Hall. Concannon found turn-of-the-century photographs of the mansion in a reference library in Kingston. Then, in a Kingston basement, he uncovered hundreds of fragments of original carved and molded wood removed from Rose Hall. He discovered other records that aided in reconstruction of the stone exterior walls, windows, and the beautiful missing mahogany stairway.

During a period of meticulous restoration, floors were replaced as was the roof. Some authentic period antiques were purchased, but much of the mahogany furniture was handcrafted in Jamaica by local artisans. In all, the project cost more than $2.5 million. Rose Hall reopened in 1971.

Since that date the dining room with its four-pedestal Sheraton table has become a favorite with visitors. The hand-painted rice paper wall covering in the room depicts 63 species of birds.

Each year thousands of visitors tour the 18th Century Great House and view the elegant chandeliers, Chinese porcelain, and ornate fabrics. They listen to the old tales of Annie Palmer and peer into dark corners in search of her ghost.

No matter what the event, Annie Palmer's presence is never far away. Even today some people refuse to remain at the Great House after dark, and some folks swear to tales of unexplained happenings—missing drink glasses and objects moved when no one else is around. Perhaps the "white witch" remains, keeping watch over Rose Hall Great House and all who visit there.

Arches on the first level of the Rose Hall Great House give it a character of its own. Wide brick walkways provide a cool retreat from Jamaican sunshine.

A handsome screen decorates part of the ballroom at Rose Hall.

The dining room at Rose Hall includes a Chinese wall covering made of rice paper that depicts 63 species of birds. George III mahogany chairs surround the Sheraton banquet table. A lovely chandelier of French Armolu and crystal hangs above the table.

Prospect Plantation is a popular side trip from resorts such as the Wyndham Rose Hall.

Dunn's River Falls is one of the most beautiful sights in all of Jamaica. Several times daily droves of tourists hold hands to make the climb along the slippery rocks within the falls' waters.

Gorgeous sunsets like those seen from Rick's Café in Negril have added to Jamaica's fame as a vacation retreat.

What Brass Plaques by Hotel Entrances Mean

Many of the hotels in *Hotels to Remember* have special brass plaques hanging by the entrance doors. Some of the hotels have more than one special distinction. The following are explanations of these designations.

Historic Hotels of America

Historic Hotels of America was founded in 1989 and in 2000 had 145 hotels in 41 states listed in its directory. Hotels included are located in historic settings, must be at least 50 years old and have "historical significance."

Hotel del Coronado, The Brown Palace Hotel, Hotel du Pont, Renaissance Vinoy Resort, Hyatt Regency St. Louis, La Fonda, The Grove Park Inn, The Homestead, The Jefferson, Williamsburg Inn, and The Pfister are all outstanding historic properties included in *Hotels to Remember.*

Preferred Hotels & Resorts Worldwide

Preferred Hotels and Resorts have a reputation of being fine independent luxury hotels and resorts. "With distinctive styles … each Preferred hotel or resort offers a unique mix of ambiance, furnishings and architecture," says Peter Cass, President and CEO.

The Brown Palace Hotel, Hotel du Pont, Keswick Hall, The Jefferson, Williamsburg Inn, and The Pfister are Preferred hotels included in *Hotels to Remember.*

Orient-Express Hotels

In 1976, the Hotel Cipriani in Venice, Italy became the first Orient-Express Hotel. James B. Sherwood, chairman and founder of Orient-Express Hotels, Trains & Cruises, says all the properties have "one unifying principle – to offer our guests the highest standard of comfort and service in a unique environment."

Keswick Hall at Monticello is one of five Orient-Express Hotels in America and is featured in *Hotels to Remember.* Charleston Place in Charleston, SC; Windsor Court Hotel, New Orleans, LA; and La Samanna in St. Martin, French West Indies will be part of *More Hotels to Remember.*

Bibliography

A Treasury of Railroad Folklore. Edited by B. A. Botkin and Alvin F. Harlow.

Adams, Ansel. An Autobiography. Little, Brown and Company, 1986.

Albright, Horace and Robert Cahn. *The Birth of the National Park Service: The Founding Years,* 1913-33. Salt Lake City, 1985.

Arteaga, Robert F., *Building of the Arch*. St. Louis: Nies/Artcraft Printing Companies, 1967.

Ayres, Harry V. *Hotel du Pont Story*. Serendipity Press, 1981.

Barnes, Christine. *Great Lodges of the West*. W.W. West, Inc., 1997.

Beal, Merrill D. *Grand Canyon: The Story Behind The Scenery*. KC Publications, Inc., 1989.

Bonechi, Casa Editrice. *Carcassonne*. Via Cairoli 18/b, Florence, Italy, 1998.

Cheng, Pang Guek, *Canada, Cultures of the World*, Marshall Cavendish, 1994.

Cohen, Stan, *The Homestead and Warm Springs Valley*. Pictorial Histories Publishing Company, 1984.

D'Emillo, Sandra and Suzan Campbell. *Visions and Visionaries: The Art and Artists of the Santa Fe Railway*. Salt Lake City: Gibbs Smith.

DeSamper, Hugh. *Welcome to the Williamsburg Inn*. Colonial Williamsburg Foundation, 1997.

Feldman, Jody S. *City-Smart Guidebook – St. Louis*.

Fisher, Leonard Everett. *Monticello*. New York: Holiday House, 1988.

Georgia O'Keeffe – One Hundred Flowers. Edited by Kate Giel, 1991.

Guttman, Peter. *Nights to Imagine*. 1996.

Hotel del Coronado. Published by Hotel del Coronado, 1984.

Hubbard, Freeman. *Encyclopedia of North American Railroading: 150 Years of Railroading in The United States and Canada*. New York, 1981.

Johnson, Bruce E. *Built for the Ages, A History of Grove Park Inn*. The Grove Park Inn and Country Club.

Laughlin, Rosemary. *The Building of the Central Pacific Railroad*. Morgan Reynolds, Inc., 1996.

May, Alan M. *The Legend of Kate Morgan: The Search for the Ghost of the Hotel del Coronado.* 1991.

McMillon, Bill. *Old Lodges and Hotels of Our National Parks.* South Bend, Ind.: Icarus Press, 1983.

Morris, Juddi. *The Harvey Girls.* Walker Publishing Company, Inc., 1994.

Murphy, Jim. *Across America on an Emigrant Train.* Houghton Mifflin, 1993.

Murphy, M'Layne. *Historic Virginia Inns.* 1986.

Neering, Rosemary. *Victoria.* Beautiful British Columbia, 1994.

New Encyclopedia of the American West. Edited by Howard R. Lamar, 1998.

Official Guide to Colonial Williamsburg. The Colonial Williamsburg Foundation, 1985.

Piedmont, Donlan. *Peanut Soup and Spoonbread: An Informal History of Hotel Roanoke.* Roanoke: Progress Press, 1994.

Richards, Norman. *Monticello.* Chicago: Children's Press, 1995.

Rogers, Barbara Radcliffe and Rogers, Stillman D., *Canada,* Children's Press, A Division of Grolier Publishing Co., Inc., 2000.

Rothery, Agnes. *Houses Virginians Have Loved.* New York: Bonanza Books, 1965.

Rose Hall, Jamaica. Edited by Rex Nettleford. Rose Hall Limited, 1973.

Taylor, L. B. *The Ghosts of Tidewater.* Progress Printing Co., Inc., 1990.

The Homestead, A Brief History, Employee Partner Introduction. Copyright 1999, The Homestead, LC.

The Pfister Art Collection, Compiled by Burton Lee Potterveld, artist and instructor at Layton School of Art under the direction of Ray Smith, Jr., former President of The Pfister Hotel, 1977.

Witherspoon, Margaret Johanson. *Remembering the St. Louis World's Fair.* St. Louis: Comfort Printing, 1973.

Wooten, Nancy Coleman. *Rose Hill.* South Carolina Wildlife, Nov.-Dec. 1991.

(I am also indebted to information and help provided by many of the hotels and communities, especially the St. Louis Convention and Visitors Commission, The Hotel del Coronado, the Renaissance Vinoy, The Pfister, and The Homestead. I have visited and personally photographed each of the locations and conducted interviews at each site.)

Colophon

Though it is most likely impossible to acknowledge the myriad of skills, efforts, and resources that combined to produce this, Oak Tree Publishing's first full-color art book, the publisher feels duty-bound to try.

First, we are grateful to the artist and author, Mary Montague Sikes, for entrusting us with the product of her vision, talent, and decade of hard work, and we salute her husband, Olen, for his unwavering support of the project.

To Daniel Farrow of Creative Marketing Concepts, Los Angeles, CA, whose role grew from marketing consultation to full-fledged project management and who brought everything into focus, kept us on track, and took creative problem solving to an art form—Huzzah!

Don Newcomb of Custom Creations, Richmond, VA provided invaluable expertise and assistance in ensuring true digital representations of the artist's work were provided to the interior designer.

Connie Jacobs of CJ Media, Montclair, CA, created a brilliant interior design—a perfect showcase for the art and a reader-friendly presentation of the text, all strung together with elegant graphic touches. In addition, Connie created a dust jacket design which has the unique distinction of pleasing all of us at the same time.

Ron Kenner, of RKedit, Los Angeles, CA provided invaluable fine-tuning and vetting of the text, as did Barbara Hoffman of Torrance, CA and Dianne Wilkins of Yorba Linda, CA.

Finally, there is another whose acknowledgment is vital. This contributor made it possible for a production team primarily in California to communicate, coordinate and share information with an artist/author in Virginia, provided the flexibility for easy-to-do preliminary layouts as well as the lovely and sophisticated finished product, made a digital galley handy so all parties could tweak simultaneously without leaving home base, and more. Available at a snap, anytime of day or night, this contributor is technology itself.

There is a certain symmetry to the realization that today's technological wizardry made it possible to preserve in book form the elegance and tradition of these classic hotels, many of which were constructed before there was electricity, not to mention computers.